BLACK&DECKER®

THE COMPLETE GUIDE TO

ROOFING
SIDING & TRIM

Creative Publishing
international

MINNEAPOLIS, MINNESOTA
www.creativepub.com

Creative Publishing
international

Copyright © 2008
Creative Publishing international, Inc.
400 First Avenue North, Suite 300
Minneapolis, Minnesota 55401
1-800-328-0590
www.creativepub.com
All rights reserved

Printed in Singapore

10 9 8 7 6 5 4 3 2 1

Library of Congress Cataloging-in-Publication Data

The complete guide to roofing, siding & trim / created by: the editors
of Creative Publishing International, Inc., in cooperation with Black &
Decker. -- Updated 2nd ed.
    p. cm.
  At head of title: Black & Decker.
  Rev. ed. of: The complete guide to roofing & siding. 2004
  Includes index.
  Summary: "Provides all the information homeowners need in order to
maintain, repair, and install all types of roofing, siding and
trim"--Provided by publisher.
  ISBN-13: 978-1-58923-418-5 (soft cover)
  ISBN-10: 1-58923-418-9 (soft cover)
  1. Roofing--Handbooks, manuals, etc. 2.
Roofing--Installation--Handbooks, manuals, etc. 3. Roofs--Maintenance
and repair--Handbooks, manuals, etc. 4. Siding (Building
materials)--Handbooks, manuals, etc. I. Creative Publishing
International. II. Black & Decker Corporation (Towson, Md.) III.
Complete guide to roofing & siding. IV. Title: Roofing, siding & trim.
V. Title: Complete guide to roofing, siding, and trim.
  TH2431.C66 2008
  695--dc22
                        2008026823

President/CEO: Ken Fund
VP for Sales & Marketing: Kevin Hamric

Home Improvement Group

Publisher: Bryan Trandem
Managing Editor: Tracy Stanley
Senior Editor: Mark Johanson
Editor: Jennifer Gehlhar

Creative Director: Michele Lanci-Altomare
Senior Design Managers: Jon Simpson, Brad Springer
Design Manager: James Kegley

Lead Photographer: Steve Galvin
Photo Coordinator: Joanne Wawra
Shop Manager: Bryan McLain
Shop Assistant: Cesar Fernandez Rodriguez

Production Managers: Linda Halls, Laura Hokkanen

Contributing Editor: Chris Marshall

Page Layout Artist: Danielle Smith
Photographer: Andrea Rugg
Shop Help: Charlie Boldt, David Hartley

Cover photo courtesy of Alcoa Home Exteriors, Inc.
www.alcoahomes.com

The Complete Guide to Roofing, Siding & Trim
Created by: The Editors of Creative Publishing international, Inc., in cooperation with Black & Decker®.
Black & Decker is a trademark of The Black & Decker Corporation and is used under license.

NOTICE TO READERS

For safety, use caution, care, and good judgment when following the procedures described in this book. The publisher and Black & Decker cannot assume responsibility for any damage to property or injury to persons as a result of misuse of the information provided.

The techniques shown in this book are general techniques for various applications. In some instances, additional techniques not shown in this book may be required. Always follow manufacturers' instructions included with products, since deviating from the directions may void warranties. The projects in this book vary widely as to skill levels required: some may not be appropriate for all do-it-yourselfers, and some may require professional help.

Consult your local building department for information on building permits, codes, and other laws as they apply to your project.

Contents

The Complete Guide to Roofing, Siding & Trim

Introduction

Your home's roof, siding, and trim form a protective envelope against the elements, but their value extends beyond that crucial goal of keeping you dry. When selected carefully and installed properly, these three systems create an important curb impression that adds value to your property, improves the neighborhood, and makes you feel proud of your home. So, whether you need to replace your aging shingles out of necessity or decide to update faded siding just to spruce the place up, your efforts usually pay dividends both functionally and aesthetically. It's hard to go wrong embarking on a roofing, siding, or exterior trim project with the right guidance.

Contrary to what you may think, you don't have to hire a contractor to tackle a roof replacement, install fiber cement siding, or hang a new soffit system. If you've got a spirit of adventure and consider yourself to be a moderate to experienced do-it-yourselfer, you have what it takes to get these projects done effectively. By doing the work yourself, you save a bundle of money in the process—and that's an enticing prospect for any homeowner on a budget. Think you're up for the challenge? Then this book, *The Complete Guide to Roofing, Siding & Trim,* is the perfect guide to get you started and walk you through every step of the process.

The first section of the book opens with an inspirational gallery of roofing and siding products installed on a variety of contemporary homes so you can begin to dream about the possibilities. The next section, Planning for New Roofing & Siding, helps you turn those dreams into reality as you plan your roofing, siding, or trim projects. The section explains how to evaluate your needs and identify current problems with your home's exterior. Then, you get an exhaustive crash course on the latest products available to you. Options for roofing, siding, and trim have never been greater, greener, and more DIY friendly than they are now. With a little time spent in this section of the book, you will get the look, performance, and value you demand. We also show you how to estimate your projects accurately as well as how to work safely at heights—a necessity for most roofing, siding, and trim projects.

The following sections focus on installing roofing, siding, masonry, and exterior trim. The thorough step-by-step instructions and insightful photography show professional installation techniques for nearly every roofing, siding, ventilation, and trim product available: asphalt shingles, metal roofing, wood shakes and shingles, tile and rolled roofing; and siding of all kinds, including stucco, veneered stone, and cement. We then explain how to install important roof and soffit ventilation and gutters. Finally, the important final touches are revealed, such as how to complete your home's exterior with window and door brickmold, build and hang shutters, and add other decorative trim details to gables, beams, and cornices.

Once your new exterior is complete, we'll show you how to extend its life and maximize your investment. In these final sections of the book, you learn how to clean, paint, and stain properly as well as how to carry out other essential repairs for roofing, siding, flashing, gutters, trim, and masonry surfaces. Even if these jobs won't be necessary for years to come, you'll be prepared to take action when they are.

Thank you for choosing *The Complete Guide to Roofing, Siding & Trim*. We hope it will be an essential reference guide for all of your exterior home improvement project needs.

Inspiration Gallery

An impressive exterior is a combination of beautiful siding, attractive roofing, and complementary trim. Well-chosen exterior products will work together to enhance the look and appeal of your home, and keep the house watertight. The "perfect" siding gives the home its personality. For example, brick siding looks imposing and robust, while vinyl siding offers a contemporary look and feel.

Roofing also affects the character of a home. Monotone asphalt shingles, for example, make a house less imposing, while a colorful metal roof can become a major decorative feature.

The inspiring photos in this section feature a wide range of roofing and siding types, styles, and materials. They're sure to generate new ideas and help you make practical decisions when choosing roofing and siding.

The clay tile roof and stucco siding complement each other on this Mediterranean-style house. The parallel lines on the roof are offset by the solid surface of the walls.

Standing seam metal roofing is a lightweight, long-lasting option that stands up well to hail, snowloads, and high winds. Despite the misconceptions you may have heard, metal roofing won't attract lightning or make your attic hotter in summer.

Brightly colored siding and shutters, combined with white window trim and a light-gray asphalt roof, give this expansive home a cheery and welcoming presence. Be sure to take your home's size and style into account when choosing a color scheme for your next siding or roofing project.

Simulated cedar vinyl shakes offer the performance of vinyl lap siding with improved appearance. They provide the look of hand-split cedar without the maintenance of real wood.

A few eye-catching exterior trim details offer one way to make your home stand out on the block. Accentuate your windows and siding with custom shutters, dentil trim, and other archictectural details. These features will add shape, texture, and color to your siding scheme.

Mortarless brick siding adds the stately beauty of brick to your home without requiring you to hire a mason. The system shown here uses a stacked, tongue-and-groove locking system that fastens to exterior walls with screws.

A splash of manufactured veneer stone, with its various colors, tones, and shapes, can set your home apart from many of today's cookie-cutter house designs. You may be the only one who knows it's not the real thing.

Concrete exterior home covering might seem like a monochromatic choice, but it actually harmonizes quite well with the exposed beams, large windows, and open styling of this home.

Log cabin siding adds rustic charm to modern structures. It can be found at most home improvement centers and is well suited for DIY installations.

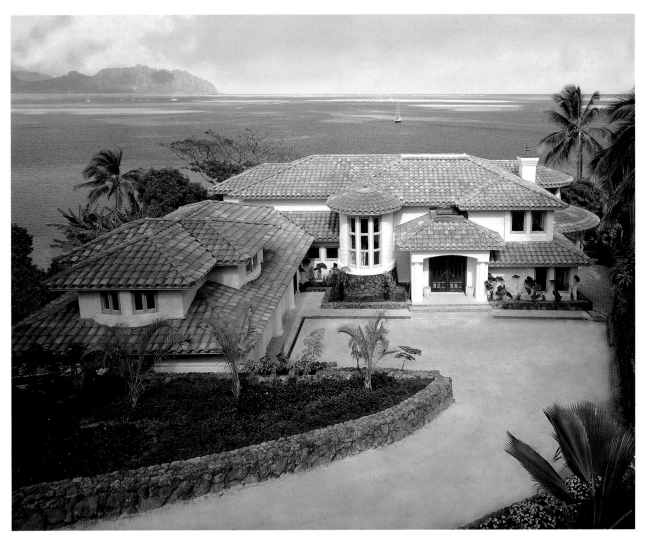

Clay tile roofing will stand up to brutal summer heat or hurricane winds beautifully. Its proven track record and attractive appearance make it one of the preferred choices for premium roofing on southern and coastal homes.

A blend of plastics, wood fibers, and tire-derived rubber combine to create these simulated cedar shakes (see Resources, page 266). In addition to being environmentally friendlier than some other roofing options, they look great on both rustic and suburban homes.

A slate roof will last a century or more, but it is costly, heavy, and difficult to install yourself. Now, you can enjoy the look of slate without its usual drawbacks if you install a simulated slate roof on your home. The tiles shown here are made of polymer molded with natural edges and deep shadowlines to mimic natural slate (see Resources).

Aluminum siding has been a popular and cost-effective option for more than 50 years. It is available in a spectrum of attractive colors and several surface textures. If you're a competent do-it-yourselfer, you can probably install it yourself for even more savings.

A tile roof, dark trim, and manufactured stone work to good effect here, giving this home a sense of permanence and security without detracting from the view beyond.

The next time you replace your home's siding, consider a synthetic stone product. It will impart the old-world charm of European cottages, and the material costs much less than natural stone.

There are several alternatives to cedar shakes among today's innovative siding options. Here, galvanized steel takes on the texture and look of wood. Steel shakes are lightweight, and you'll never need to paint them. They install with ordinary hand tools.

Soffits and fascia seal the ends and underside of your roof from wind-driven rain and animal pests while providing an important form of roof ventilation. Soffit systems are available for all types of vinyl and metal siding, and wood siding often features wood soffits built from standard lumber or sheet stock. Any full-scale siding project should also include soffit and fascia treatments. See pages 180 to 192 for more information on soffits, fascia and venting.

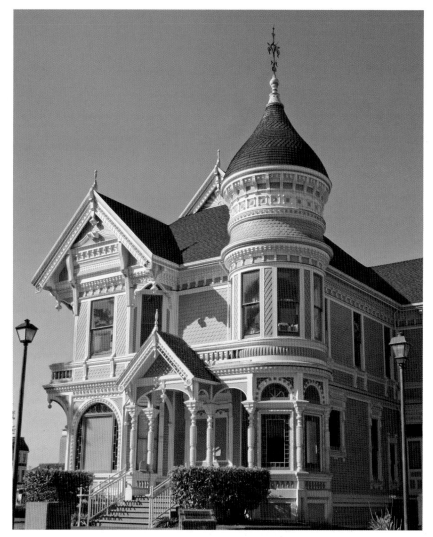

A combination of ornate trim details, siding textures, and, of course, splendid architecture, makes this Queen Anne Victorian timeless. Here was the heyday of exterior home detailing with wood shingle siding, contrasting diagonal siding used around windows and on gable ends, and a variety of cast on spindling and detailing. You can still see many of these design details incorporated into today's homes of a more modest scale. In the classic Queen Anne, the design goal was to avoid any flat wall surfaces, and such a project would represent a DIY masterpiece.

Roofing, siding, and trim are the outer layer of an integrated protective system that seals your house. Not only do they function as a working network, they should blend together nicely in style, color, and scale. The exterior treatment on this house is a good example of a well-executed exterior system, where styles of roofing, siding and trim present an attractive modern version of a classic farmhouse style.

Planning for New Roofing & Siding

Roofing, siding, and exterior trim details create the outer envelope of your home, safeguarding it from the elements. Aside from their protective purposes, these three systems should also blend together aesthetically to improve your home's appearance. Roofing and siding replacement, in particular, are among the more costly projects you'll face as a homeowner, and generally they're investments you'll make only every few decades or so. For these reasons, it's wise to plan your projects carefully, so you can keep all the relevant factors in mind before you begin.

This chapter will help you get started on the right foot. You'll begin the planning process by evaluating your needs and estimating both price and material quantities required for the job. Then, you'll take a more in-depth look at the wide variety of product options available. New forms and styles of roofing and siding continue to come to market, and there may be some you simply aren't aware of yet. A roofing, siding, or trim project will usually require at least some work at heights. You'll learn important tips for working safely, how to set up scaffolds, and how to prepare your job site to minimize damage, manage debris, and work efficiently.

In this chapter:
- Evaluating Your Needs
- Choosing Roofing & Siding
- Estimating Roofing & Siding
- Working Safely
- Setting Up Scaffolding
- Pump-Jack Scaffolding
- Installing Roof Jacks

Evaluating Your Needs

There are many good reasons to replace roofing or siding—it may be leaking, reaching the end of its life span, or look sorely out of date. These reasons will probably change as your roofing and siding age. Or, you may just decide one day that your home needs a facelift, and you want to replace the roofing or siding with something more lively.

Before jumping right into a replacement project, ensure that your new roofing or siding will meet all of your objectives. If you like the look and style of your shingles but they're getting old, it's a simple matter to replace them with a newer version. On the other hand, if you're tired of maintaining your siding, you'll want a product that looks nice but doesn't require constant attention.

Also consider your future needs. If you're replacing your siding now and will need to replace your roofing in a few years, plan now for a siding that will complement the new roof. If you're installing a new soffit and fascia system, it's a good time to install the gutters you've always needed. It's often easier to replace all materials at once rather than doing it piecemeal.

In some cases, you may not need to replace your roofing or siding to achieve your goals. Adding shutters or painting your trim a vibrant color can brighten up your exterior. Some basic maintenance can increase the life span of your roofing and siding. If you notice leaks on your ceilings or walls, don't automatically assume the roofing or siding needs replacing. Sometimes, flashing or caulking is all that's needed.

The following pages show common exterior problems. If some of these look familiar, evaluate your house to determine what's needed to fix the problem.

Your roofing and siding should meet the two fundamental needs of making your home look attractive and protecting it from the elements.

Identifying Roofing and Siding Problems

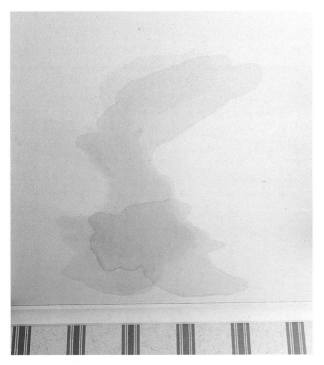

Ceiling stains show up on interior surfaces, but they're usually caused by leaks in the roof.

When shingles start to cup or show signs of widespread damage they need to be replaced.

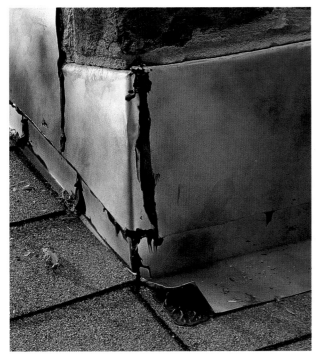

Loose flashing can be caused by external forces, such as high winds, or by the failure of the sealant or fasteners. The flashing can usually be repaired or replaced without replacing the shingles.

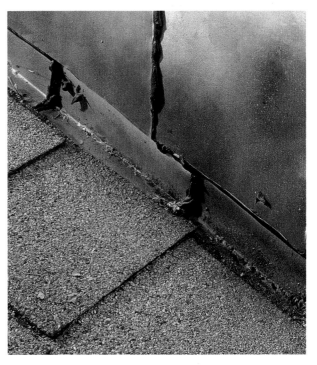

Damaged and deteriorated flashing can cause roof leaks. The damaged piece or pieces need to be removed and replaced.

(continued)

Blistering or peeling paint can be scraped off, then the wood can be painted.

Damaged panels of siding can be removed and replaced; you don't need to replace the entire siding. The new panels are then painted to match the surrounding ones.

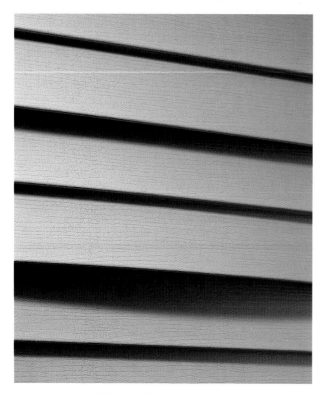

Manufactured siding buckles when it's nailed incorrectly or when the expansion gaps are too small to allow for adequate movement. The siding needs to be removed and either renailed or trimmed to the proper size, then reinstalled.

Surface damage to metal siding is difficult to repair, and cosmetic repairs often look worse than the damage. If the damage is widespread, the siding will need to be replaced.

Rot and pest damage are the primary enemies of soffits. Small spots of damage can be repaired by replacing the damaged area. Widespread damage will require a new soffit system.

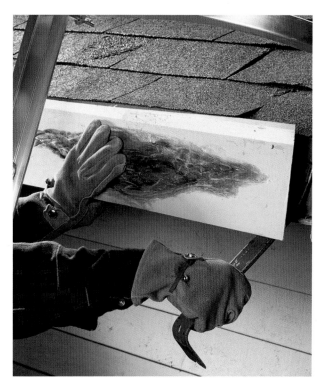

Rotten fascia is easy to spot from the ground on homes without a gutter system. If your house has gutters, check behind them for rot, especially if the gutters are sagging.

Leaking gutters usually result from holes or separated joints. Leaky joints can be caulked and reassembled, and holes can be patched.

Damaged gutter sections should be patched or replaced. If the damage is widespread, replace the entire gutter system.

Choosing Roofing & Siding

With so many options, choosing a roofing or siding material for your home can seem like a daunting task. Appearance, cost, ease of installation, life span, value, and maintenance all play a role. Prioritize what factors are important to you, and make your decisions accordingly. Are you willing to pay more for a cedar shake roof, or will you be content with a less-expensive asphalt shingle that imitates shakes? Are you willing to paint your wood siding every 7 to 10 years, or do you prefer a maintenance-free exterior?

Even after you've narrowed your decision down to a type of material, you'll still need to choose a style and color. For example, asphalt roofing is available in a seemingly endless number of colors and styles, from red scallops to green dimensional to gray three-tab shingles. Vinyl siding colors are constantly changing, and the styles range from Dutch lap to double 3" clapboard, to shakes, to board and batten.

Architectural features on the house, and even other materials already installed on the house, can help in your decision making. Stucco siding and clay roofing are a natural fit. Brick siding and metal roofing complement each other. Vinyl siding and asphalt shingles are a popular combination.

Because most roof and siding materials last for decades, you'll be living with your decision for a very long time. Take your time looking at different products, weighing their advantages and any disadvantages, before finalizing your decision.

Price: For most homeowners, the cost of materials is one of the deciding factors in selecting roofing or siding.

Prices are as varied as the products themselves and can differ from region to region. When adding up the costs for your project, consider everything you'll need to complete the job—not just the main roofing or siding materials. In most cases, you'll also need to purchase flashing, trim, and fasteners.

Depending on your tool arsenal, you may need to buy new tools. Some installation processes require specialty tools that you probably wouldn't otherwise have. If you're installing clay roofing, you'll need a diamond saw blade. For brick or stucco siding, mason's tools are needed. Shipping and delivery charges, and special-order costs can also impact your budget. Find out about these costs before settling on a product.

Slate, clay, and copper are generally the most expensive roofing products, followed by metal, cedar shakes and shingles, organic asphalt, fiberglass asphalt, and then roll roofing. Brick and stone are at the high end of the siding price scale, followed by stucco, fiber cement, wood shakes and shingles, wood lap, and vinyl, in that order.

If you're married to a particular look but can't afford the real thing, consider less expensive substitutes. The look and features of many premium roofing and siding products are now replicated in other materials. Some metal roofs mimic the more expensive slate, and some asphalt shingles look like the higher priced wood shakes. For siding, one of the least-expensive products—vinyl—is now designed to imitate wood lap, wood shingles, or wood scallops. In some cases, just changing the species of wood can save a significant cost. For example, log cabin siding in pine is much more affordable than the same cabin siding in cedar.

It's important to shop around and compare prices. Visit distribution centers, lumberyards, and home improvement stores to find the best deals.

Price Comparison ▶

	Roofing	Siding
Most Expensive	Slate	Brick
	Clay	Stone
	Copper	Stucco
Least Expensive	Metal	Fiber cement
	Cedar shakes/shingles	Wood shakes
	Asphalt	Wood shingles
	Roll roofing	Wood lap
		Vinyl

Cost is only one aspect of choosing new roofing or siding. Be sure to keep the other relevant factors of ease of installation, life span, maintenance, and of course, appearance, in mind, too.

Color and texture should complement one another when you choose siding and roofing materials. This does not mean that they need to match exactly. In fact, the most successful pairings offer some contrast. Here, natural cedar shingles are installed on the walls and finished with a warm semi-transparent wood stain. This blends well with the architectural shingles and their gradations of brown tones. Even the addition of a third element, the natural brick veneer on the steps and foundation, succeeds because it shares a palette with both the roofing and siding and has a textural similarity to the asphalt roof shingles.

Maintenance Considerations

The amount of maintenance each product requires is another important factor when choosing roofing and siding materials. Some products are virtually maintenance free, while others require regular upkeep. Decide how much time and effort you're willing to invest in maintaining your roofing and siding, and purchase materials that meet your criteria.

Maintenance tends to be more of a factor for siding than for roofing. The thought of having to paint the exterior every 7 to 10 years turns a lot of homeowners away from wood siding products. For others, painting is an opportunity to change the color of the house every decade or so. The amount of maintenance a siding requires is not necessarily reflected in its cost, since products at both ends of the price scale—brick at the high end and vinyl at the low end—need little or no maintenance.

Older types of stucco were known to chip and crack and they needed regular maintenance. Today's stucco products use epoxy, eliminating the chipping and cracking. If the final coat of stucco is tinted to the color you want, you won't even have to paint it. Once it's installed, stucco rarely needs any maintenance. Brick and stone sidings also require little maintenance, although the mortar joints may eventually need to be filled with new mortar. Likewise, vinyl siding is maintenance free, which is part of its appeal.

Wood siding products need the most attention. A coat of paint, stain, or sealer is usually needed every 7 to 10 years, and that task involves a lot of preparation work, such as scraping and sanding. Fiber cement siding also needs to be repainted, but not as often. The standard time frame between paint jobs is 15 years.

In general, maintenance for roofing materials is fairly minimal. It's usually the result of damage to roofing components, such as torn or cracked shingles, or a break in the metal flashing. Metal, tile, and clay roofs will probably never need any maintenance. Individual asphalt shingles and wooden shakes and shingles periodically become loose, in which case they can simply be renailed. Roll roofing can develop blisters or small holes, which can be repaired with roofing cement and patches of roll roofing.

All roofing and siding products can benefit from an occasional cleaning. This helps keep the exterior looking its best and enables you to identify potential trouble areas.

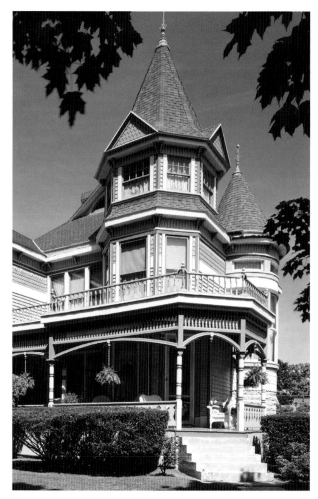

Vinyl siding and asphalt shingles require very little maintenance. They can be used on any type of home, including this Victorian.

Siding Maintenance ▸

Material (Siding)	Maintenance	Type of Maintenance
Vinyl	Low	Occasional cleaning
Brick	Low	Filling mortar joints
Stone	Low	Filling mortar joints
Stucco	Low	Fix cracks/chips
Fiber cement	Medium	Painting
Wood shakes	Medium	Painting/staining
Wood shingles	Medium	Painting/staining
Wood lap	High	Painting

Durability

Consider the life span of the products that you want to install on your roof or exterior walls. Some materials are extremely durable and guaranteed to last 50 years or more, while others need to be replaced in as few as 12 years.

The longevity of some products is influenced by your geographic location. Salt air along the coasts has been notoriously damaging to wood siding products, and areas subjected to high winds are prone to roofing and siding materials blowing off. The way you care for your exterior also impacts its longevity. If you regularly paint your wood siding, immediately repair any roofing or siding damage, and follow the manufacturer's guidelines for each product, the materials will last longer.

Roofing: Slate, concrete, and clay tile are the most durable roofing products. They're heavier than other materials, and usually have a lifetime warranty. Some slate and clay roofs have been known to last hundreds of years. Metal roofs, despite their light weight, are remarkably durable. Warranties vary by product and manufacturer, but warranties of 50 years or more are becoming standard.

Since wood shakes are available in different grades, their durability also differs. Top-quality shakes carry 50-year warranties, while the lower-end shakes last about 30 years. The life span of asphalt shingles also widely varies. They should last a minimum of 20 years, with the thicker, more durable architectural shingles guaranteed for up to 50 years. Roll roofing has the shortest life span, lasting between 6 and 12 years.

Siding: Brick is generally considered the most durable product, and it can carry a warranty of more than 100 years. Stone and stucco sidings are also noted for their durability, and they generally carry 50-year warranties. Standard warranties for fiber cement siding are 50 years, too.

Although the life span of wood siding varies, depending on the species of wood, climate conditions, and amount of homeowner maintenance it receives, you should expect wood siding to last a minimum of 20 years. Some wood sidings can last well over 50 years. Vinyl siding is available in different thicknesses, from 0.035" to 0.055", with the thicker siding being the more durable and carrying lifetime warranties. The lighter-weight vinyl sidings are usually guaranteed to last between 30 and 50 years.

Asphalt shingles and vinyl siding are a popular combination due to their low cost and good durability. Both products last 20 to 50 years.

Brick is the most durable siding, and it can last over 100 years with little or no maintenance.

Asphalt Three-Tab Shingles

Asphalt three-tab roof shingles consist of a sandwich of asphalt and fiberglass or felt layers covered by mineral granules. For several important reasons they've been the dominant roofing option in the United States for more than a century. Weighing 2 to 3 pounds per square foot, asphalt shingles are relatively lightweight compared to slate, clay, or cement tile. Any pitched roof that's suitable for shingling (a 4-in-12 slope or greater) and properly constructed can accept asphalt shingles without further reinforcement.

Asphalt three-tabs are reasonably priced, and you can expect them to last from 8 to 30 years, depending on the quality of the shingle. Installing or repairing asphalt shingles isn't difficult; in fact, it's the most approachable roofing material for do-it-yourselfers or any qualified roofing installer. Ease of installation also helps keep costs down. Once installed, high-quality asphalt singles are relatively maintenance free and offer good fire and wind resistance. They come in a wide range of colors to blend in nicely with any siding and trim color scheme. If you live in a damp or coastal environment, you can also find asphalt shingles impregnated with algaecides to prevent unsightly staining.

The most common roof covering by far, asphalt three-tab shingles are inexpensive, lightweight, and available in a wide range of colors and styles. They are also easy to install.

Asphalt Shingle Types ▸

3-tab

Architectural shingles

25-year rating

Shadow-line shingles

4-tabs

Asphalt shingles are usually rated by life span, with 20-, 25-, and 40-year ratings the most common (although some now claim to be 50-year shingles). Functionally, these ratings should be used for comparison purposes only. In fact, the average life span of an asphalt shingle roof in the United States is 8 to 10 years.

The term "multitab shingle" refers to any asphalt shingle manufactured with stamped cutouts to mimic the shapes of slate tile or wood shakes. Multitab cutouts are made and installed in single-thickness, 3-ft. strips, so these tabbed reveals show up. The ubiquitous term for them is "three-tab," but two- and four-tab styles are also available. Generally, the tabs are spaced evenly along each sheet of shingle to provide a uniform appearance and a stepped, bricklaid pattern on the roof. However, some manufacturers also offer styles with shaped corners or randomly spaced tabs trimmed to different heights for a more unique look.

Laminated Asphalt Shingles

Laminated asphalt shingles are an increasingly popular option for new homes or roofing replacements. You may also hear them referred to as "dimensional," "architectural," or "multithickness" shingles. Essentially, laminated asphalt shingles have the same material composition as multitab cutout shingles—a sandwich of asphalt, base sheeting of felt or fiberglass, and granular coatings. However, the important difference is that instead of a single shingle layer, two layers are bonded together to create a three-dimensional appearance. The top layer has wide, randomly sized notches, and it overlays a staggered, unnotched bottom layer. The effect of this lamination treatment helps mimic the natural inconsistencies of a cedar shake or slate roof.

Laminated shingles are no more difficult to install than three-tab shingles, and the same installation methods apply. The random pattern can even reduce overall installation waste because the pattern is more visually forgiving than the uniform design of three-tab shingles. Sections of shingle that would otherwise interrupt a three-tab pattern can still be used in a laminated shingle installation.

The added shingle layer makes laminated shingles heavier than standard three-tab shingles, but the weight difference isn't critical; any pitched roof can accept them without special structural reinforcement. Laminated shingles are also thicker than multitab shingles, which gives them improved wind resistance and durability. As you might expect, they're more expensive than three-tab shingles. The added thickness enables manufacturers to offer longer 30- to 50-year warranties, which can make them a better investment than three-tab shingles over the life of your roof.

Architectural shingles (also called laminated and dimensional) are installed very similarly to regular three-tab asphalt shingles, but they offer a more sophisticated appearance with greater visual depth. They also come with longer warranties than comparable three-tab shingles.

Asphalt Roll Roofing

For low-pitched roofs, or in cases where budgetary concerns are more important than appearance, rolled roofing might be the perfect choice for your situation. Roll roofing is also a good option if you need to cover a roof for an extended period but plan to install the final roofing at a later date.

Think of asphalt-and-granule roll roofing as continuous strips of asphalt shingles without the tab cutouts. Roll asphalt roofing is installed in overlapping layers just like asphalt shingles, but the amount of exposure from one layer to the next is much greater than it is with roll shingles. Depending on the product, asphalt roll roofing will either be entirely covered with granules and installed to provide a single layer of coverage, or only half the sheet will be covered in a granule layer. The uncoated half (called a selvedge edge) and half of the shingle layer above it are covered with roofing cement for an improved seal. The wider overlap provided by the selvedge edge lends a double-coverage effect. (Double-coverage roofing is rapidly becoming rare.)

Single-coverage roll roofing may also have a selvedge edge for cement, but it will be only a few inches wide. Single- and double-coverage styles are secured with roofing nails around the edges. Both types are suitable for do-it-yourself roofing.

Asphalt roll roofing can prove to be more "leakproof" than conventional shingles if it's installed correctly. However, it generally does not last as long as shingles. The fact that fewer nails are used during installation makes it more prone to blowing off in high winds, and it doesn't respond to thermal expansion and contraction as well as shingles. And, for most viewers, it lacks the pleasing curb appeal of a shingled roof.

Roll roofing is essentially building paper with a granular surface coating. Single-coverage roll roofing is typically installed in a perimeter bond application with an overlap of about 6". Self-adhesive ice membrane is a roll roof product that can be used for a full roof or as a preventer of ice dams in shingled roofs.

Asphalt roll roofing is one of the most inexpensive roof covering materials and when fully bonded, it's one of the very few options available for covering roofs with a low slope between 2-in-12 and 4-in-12. It cannot be used on perfectly level roofs, though. Roll roofing is a common choice for the roof of porches, sheds, and garages.

EPDM Rubber Roofing

Rubber membrane roofing, also known as ethylene propylene diene monomer (EPDM) roofing, is installed in wide sheets using a specialized latex bonding adhesive, but it is not nailed in place. Often, rubber roofs are fully bonded to the roof deck with cement, and the absence of nails makes it an even better choice for low-pitch roofs that are susceptible to leaks. You may choose to install a rubber membrane on a pitched roof simply because it is seamless and easy to install, requiring only a perimeter bond if you are mechanically fastening strips.

The membrane is available in 10- or 20-ft.-wide rolls to help reduce the total number of seams. In recent years, EPDM membrane has become more do-it-yourself friendly, and it's available to consumers through roofing suppliers and some home centers. It is comparably priced to quality asphalt shingles. However, EPDM's black color won't win any beauty contests, and it will be the hottest roof around in mid-summer's heat.

Rubber membrane roofs used to be installed exclusively in commercial situations, but DIY-friendly versions have become common in recent years. They're an excellent choice for flat or near-flat roofs.

Slate Shingles

Slate roofing has been around for centuries, and it's one of the most weather-resistant and beautiful options you can put on your roof. It is quarried and cut into thin individual shingles and installed with nails. Natural variations in color, pattern, and edge shape give slate an organic and tactile quality that's simply unmatched by other synthetic roofing products.

However, despite its visual appeal and long-lasting performance—more than 100 years in many cases—a number of important factors may make slate unfeasible for your home. For one, slate is heavy, weighing about twice as much as asphalt singles per square foot. It's also about triple the cost of premium asphalt shingles. A conventionally framed or truss roof may require additional framing before it's suitable for slate shingles. Check with a structural engineer to see if your home's roof will support slate.

Installing slate shingles involves the use of specialized cutting tools and skills, which makes it extremely complicated to install for do-it-yourselfers as well as many roofers. Once installed, slate's durability to the elements doesn't extend to foot traffic. The shingles are brittle and can break if they are stepped on. Replacing broken shingles involves installing extra staging and ladders to prevent further damage, and removing individual shingles is a complicated process.

Slate roofs are expensive and not DIY-friendly, but for overall attractiveness and durability, they're hard to beat.

Clay Tile

Clay tile roofs are common on southern and coastal homes, where intense heat and high winds are a concern. Since clay is a manufactured product, roofing tiles are available in a wide range of shapes, sizes, and colors. Clay tiles offer excellent durability and fire resistance. However, clay is slightly heavier than slate, and installing it over typical roof framing may require adding structural reinforcements. Of course, this adds to the project costs.

Depending on the region you live in, there may be many qualified roofers who can install it properly. Working with clay tile requires cutting with a diamond-blade saw, and it may not be suitable for complex roof designs. It is also relatively fragile and can not be walked on, so repairs can be difficult. The installed cost of clay tiles is comparable to slate. On all but the most basic roof designs, clay tile is not do-it-yourself friendly.

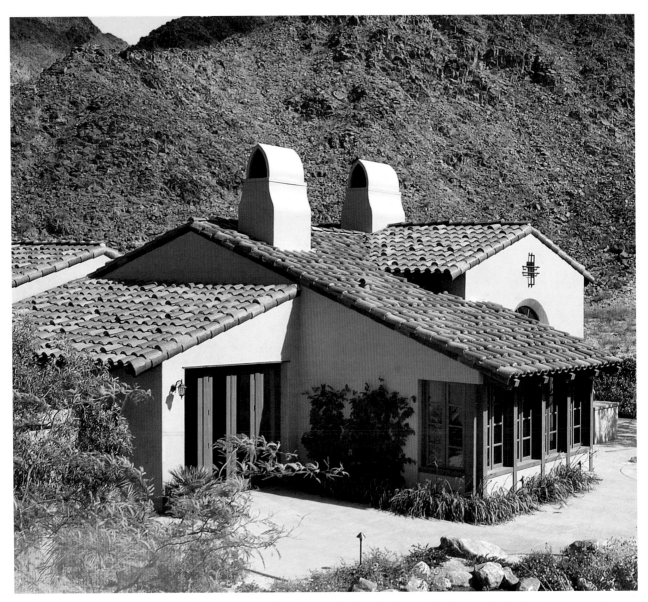

Clay tile roofs have a distinctive regional appearance, but they can be installed in practically any climate. They're heavy and relatively expensive. Most clay tiles have a half-pipe shape and terra-cotta color, but with a little research you can find a rather wide range of colors and styles.

Concrete Tile

Over the past few decades, concrete has continued to gain momentum in the roofing field. It weathers well; offers excellent wind, hail, and fire resistance; and installs similarly to clay tile and slate. Concrete is typically formed into flat shakes instead of contoured tiles, like clay, but you can special-order contoured shapes made from cement. Some manufacturers offer concrete shakes that mimic the color and texture of wood.

As you might expect, concrete shakes are heavy. They're slightly heavier than slate and about the same weight as clay tile. However, there are also concrete shakes that are fortified with wood fibers and polymers to cut down on overall weight without compromising durability. Compared with clay or slate, concrete offers similar performance characteristics with a lower overall installation cost: it's about half the price of slate or clay.

Fiber cement is growing quickly as a concrete roofing tile material, much as it is for lap siding. It offers a singular package of durability, low maintenance, beauty, and reasonable cost. Cement tiles and fiber-cement tiles usually have a simulated wood grain appearance to resemble wood shingles, but concrete tiles can be ordered in many other configurations that are less well known.

Metal Roofing

Metal roofing has proven its durability as a residential roofing material for centuries in Europe, but until recently it was more common to see a metal roof on an agricultural or commercial building than on a home here in the States. That trend is quickly changing. Advances in metal-forming techniques and improvements in coatings have created a wide variety of styles and colors to choose from, making metal roofing a more enticing option for homeowners. In fact, metal roofing is the fastest growing segment of the residential roofing products market for several reasons. For one, metal is the lightest-weight roofing material made. At around 1 to 2 pounds per square foot, any standard-framed roof can easily support metal roofing. Provided the shingles are in sound condition and local building codes permit it, metal roofing can even be installed over a layer or two of asphalt shingles. This saves on the cost and effort involved with a tearoff.

Metal offers excellent wind and fire resistance, and improvements in rust-inhibitive coatings make it weather well for many decades. It resists peeling, chalking, and fading from UV light. Metal roofs are quite common in coastal areas that are subjected to tropical storms and high winds. It also performs favorably when subjected to heavy snowfall or ice accumulations.

Prefab Panels ▶

Prefabricated panels made of metal, fiberglass, or clear polycarbonate come in standard widths and lengths and are usually installed over a system of purlins. Historically, they have been used most often to roof outbuildings and shelters, but the metal versions are becoming more popular for whole houses and room additions.

Standing-seam steel roofs are lightweight, very durable, and only moderately expensive. Typically, they are fabricated on-site by pros, but some prefabricated panel systems are DIY friendly.

A copper roof has all the advantages of steel but will not rust. Copper oxidizes over time and can corrode, but it is generally a superior exterior metal.

Unlike wood or asphalt roofing, metal will not rot, crack, or promote algae growth, so it is largely maintenance free. Light-colored metal roofs, which reflect sunlight instead of absorb it, offer energy-saving benefits as well. Attics stay cooler in summer months, which reduces energy costs. Given its durability, warranties in the 30- to 50-year range are common for professionally installed metal roofing systems. In terms of cost, metal is more expensive than premium asphalt shingles but cheaper than slate or clay.

Residential metal roofing is available in steel, aluminum, or copper. It is embossed in several surface textures to simulate clay tiles, wood shakes, or asphalt shingles. Some products are coated with granules to enhance their texture. Embossed metal roofing comes in either horizontal panels with several shingles formed on each panel or as individual shake or tile shapes. Each piece has flanges that clip to the top and bottom of adjacent pieces or nail-down clips along the edges. Smooth panels with standing seams crimped or clipped together along both long edges are the most common style of metal roofing. The metal panels can be formed on location with common metalworking tools. They're also available in prefabricated panels. Copper is most often installed in panel form and left unfinished to weather to a green patina. It is the most expensive option. Steel or aluminum roofing come in a spectrum of colors to suit any siding color scheme.

There are a few drawbacks to metal roofing worth noting. It is slippery when wet and it can be dented or scratched. Metal can be difficult to adapt to complex roof styles. Eventually steel roofing will need to be repainted to prevent corrosion.

Although it shouldn't be difficult to find qualified installers in most regions, you need special metalworking skills to tackle most residential metal roofing products yourself. Do-it-yourself installation may also void the manufacturer's warranty, so this is a project better left to the pros.

Environmentally Friendly Roofs

A little-known but new breed of environmentally friendly roofing products is now available for residential applications. If you like the look of slate, tile, or wood shakes, you can now buy them made from blends of polymers, sawdust, rubber, vinyl, and fiberglass. These composite shingles are quite flexible, so they can withstand high winds, hail damage, or foot traffic without splitting, rotting, or breaking. Fire retarders and UV inhibitors are added to make them as durable as conventional roofing options. In polymer-based shingles, the color is blended through the material, so scratches won't show and peeling isn't a concern. Some of these alternative roofing products are made from recycled materials, such as used car tires or post-industrial waste, and the roofing may be entirely recyclable when it wears out.

Polymer or rubber composite roofing materials are heavier than metal but they are about the same weight as laminated asphalt shingles. Most come with 50-year warranties that can be transferred from one homeowner to the next. They install easily with nails over typical felt underlayment, just like asphalt shingles. You may be able to install a composite roof yourself, depending on the product.

Green products on the roof, as in every other part of the house, are beginning to flood the market. This welcome occurrence is creating a whole new category of options for homeowners with pro-environment priorities. Most of the newer products, like those seen above, are made with recycled materials using composite technologies. Others, however, feature slightly older technology (see Living Roofs, next page). Local tile materials (from within a 500-mile project radius) manufactured with indigenous materials and postindustrial recycled content, including fly ash and slag, are shown here. These criteria contribute toward third party certification and possible leadership in energy and evironmental design (LEED) credits.

Living Roofs ▸

The living roof covered with plants and planting media (also called a green roof) is a rapidly advancing technology that is making a lot of news in commercial architecture, but hasn't quite found its place around the house—at least not in North America. Recently, some enterprising folks have begun to make great strides in adapting the technology to the home, including the most-frequently flat residential roof: the garage.

The benefits of a green roof are many:

- Properly maintained, they are rated to last 50 years.
- Green roofs reduce the amount of stormwater runoff, which takes pressure off sewage treatment plants.
- If the roof covers a heated and cooled space, a green roof adds insulation in the winter and can reduce your cooling costs by as much as 25 percent.
- Green roofs improve air quality: a two-car garage with a green roof will create enough oxygen annually to supply 25 people for a year.
- They add natural beauty to your property and may even support certain types of food gardening.
- A green roof can provide habitat for wildlife in an urban setting.

There are three primary methods of achieving a green roof. The first is to hire a design-and-build firm that specializes in the installation of living roofs. The second is to build one yourself using a proprietary kit-type system. Lastly, you can make one almost exclusively from products you can purchase at building and garden centers.

Here are some planning tips to consider if you're contemplating adding a green roof on your property:

- Avoid slopes greater than 2-in-12. It is not impossible to create a green roof on a steeper pitch, but it is much more complicated.
- Consult with your local building department and a structural engineer to make sure your roof structure is adequate to support the weight. A green roof will add from 10 to 100 pounds of weight per square foot, depending on how the roof is constructed and used.
- Unless your current roof covering is a waterproof membrane such as EPDM rubber or bonded PVC sheets, you will need to reroof with one of these materials (rubber is preferred).
- Depending on what plantings you choose, you will need to do occasional maintenance such as weeding and watering. If you are not comfortable working at heights, you probably should avoid green roofs.

Houses with a green roof are more common in Europe than in North America, but the many benefits they offer are spurring interest worldwide. The number of houses or garages with a living roof is growing quickly in the United States and Canada.

Vinyl & Metal Siding

Vinyl, aluminum, and steel siding were developed in the 1950s and 1960s and have been mass-produced for residential housing ever since. Chances are, most of the homes in your neighborhood are covered in one of these three types of siding. Consider the performance characteristics of each type when choosing new siding for your home.

Since siding is such a competitive market, the price of vinyl or metal siding is about the same. All three siding types are nailed in place along the top edge, with sections interlocking from one row to the next. Vinyl, aluminum, and steel can be installed by a do-it-yourselfer, but both aluminum and steel siding require the use of metal brakes and other sheet-metal tools to cut and form the siding correctly. Most homeowners find that installing metal siding is difficult to accomplish with acceptable results. Vinyl is much more DIY friendly. It can be cut easily with ordinary snips, circular saws, and utility knives.

A variety of special detailing components for wrapping windows, doors, and faucets or outlets are widely available at home centers.

Of the three types, vinyl siding dominates the residential siding market for several reasons. It is manufactured in hundreds of colors, so finding the "perfect" color for your home should be easy. The color is blended through the plastic, so scuffs or scratches will not leave noticeable blemishes. Vinyl is also molded in many surface textures and styles, including traditional or Dutch lap, scallops, shingles, fish scale, shakes, and various beaded designs. This diversity allows vinyl siding to complement historical homes and to provide design options for traditional and even eclectic homes. Vinyl is impervious to insects, rot, and fungal or algal growth, and it stands up well to moderate impact. It does not require routine cleaning or painting, and replacing sections of damaged vinyl is a fairly simple process.

Vinyl siding is very popular because it is inexpensive, low maintenance, easy to install, and widely available in many styles and colors (usually on the lighter side of the color spectrum).

Metal siding is usually made of steel these days, but in the past, aluminum and tin have been common materials. Typically, it has a baked enamel finish.

The main drawback to vinyl is that it expands and contracts with changes in temperature more than other materials. If it's improperly nailed or installed without correct expansion gaps, the siding may buckle or sag. Vinyl also shows end seams from one piece to the next—and these can be unsightly, making a house look plasticized. Still, for durability and appearance's sake, vinyl is hard to beat. Most varieties of top-quality vinyl come with lifetime, transferable warranties (allowing the warranty to transfer from one homeowner to the next).

Aluminum and steel siding are manufactured in lap styles as well as several embossed surface patterns. Metal siding has a factory-applied, high-performance coating available in many colors. Steel siding is also galvanized for greater protection against corrosion. The rigidity of steel and aluminum siding ensures a strength that vinyl cannot match: steel and aluminum will not buckle, sag, or distort. Some manufacturers now offer seamless steel and aluminum siding, which is machine-extruded by the installer on location. Each panel can be custom fit to

wall lengths to avoid the staggered seam appearance of vinyl.

There are a few drawbacks to metal siding. Unlike vinyl, which is reasonably flexible and resilient to impacts, both steel and aluminum siding can be dented by the wayward baseball, rock, or falling tree branch. Since the surface of steel and aluminum is coated and the color does not permeate the metal, it is not resistant to scratches. Steel siding can rust if its cut edges are exposed to moisture. Sunlight can degrade the painted finish on aluminum siding over time, which leaves a chalky residue that occasionally needs washing. Both aluminum and steel siding may be painted, and you can repaint as needed without special preparation techniques.

Metal siding is a relatively green choice among the siding options. A percentage of the metal in most new steel or aluminum siding comes from recycled material and, depending on the finish coating, the siding may be recyclable when you replace it. Your supplier should be able to provide you with this information before you buy.

Wood Siding

Wood siding is another viable option for your home. Clapboard or shiplap siding is typically milled from cedar, cypress, redwood, or treated southern pine. All offer excellent resistance to decay and insects. Clapboard siding is usually manufactured with a tapered edge to create the proper overlap, and it's installed horizontally. Board-and-batten wood siding can be accomplished with ordinary lumber; it's arranged vertically with a narrower wood strip that overlaps the seams between the boards. Wood siding will generally cost more than vinyl or metal, and it's prone to the same problems as wood shingles and shakes. Prolonged wetness will eventually lead to decay, and the wood will fade to gray unless you're diligent about painting or staining every few years.

Wood lap siding is still a popular choice for homes, though vinyl, wood, aluminum, steel and fiber cement reproductions are increasingly used.

Shingles & Shakes

Wood shingles and shakes on your roof or on your walls add a warm, natural look. Wood has been used this way for centuries with excellent success. These days, shingles and shakes are made from various species of cedar and cypress; white oak; and pressure-treated yellow southern pine. The wood is graded in No. 1 and premium grades, based on clarity and cut. Premium is the highest grade. It costs slightly more than premium laminated asphalt shingles.

The principal difference between wood shakes and shingles is how they are cut and processed. Shakes are more rustic than shingles. They're sawn or hand split in varying thicknesses and lengths. These irregularities give shakes an organic appeal, but they increase the chances for water infiltration if the wall and roof sheathing is not properly flashed and wrapped.

Shingles are manufactured to specific sizes and thicknesses, and they have a tapered edge. They are never hand split. Shingles can be ordered with sanded, smooth surfaces or left with the natural woodgrain texture.

A competent do-it-yourselfer can install shakes or shingles without special skills, and the material can be cut and installed with ordinary shop tools. Wood can be walked on, is abrasion resistant, and easy to repair. However, the natural color will fade to gray over time unless it is painted. Shingles and shakes must be kept clean and dry to deter fungal or algal growth and insect pests. Woodpeckers and squirrels can wreak havoc with shingles and shakes when they're looking for a quick meal or a warm place to spend the winter. For all these reasons, you should expect to carry out more maintenance tasks on wood shingles and shakes than metal, vinyl, or other synthetic options.

Wood shingles and shakes can be used on the walls of your home as well as on roofs. Shakes have a more rustic appearance than shingles because they are irregular widths.

Board & Batten Siding

For a traditional look, a board and batten appearance can be recreated with 4 × 8 sheets of exterior-rated plywood that have a textured surface and a pattern of grooves to simulate the look of individual boards (called T1-11). Grooves are spaced either 4 or 8 inches apart. The edges of the sheets have overlapping tongues that hide the seams and help keep water out. Installation is easy for a competent homeowner with basic woodworking skills, and the material costs are about the same as vinyl siding.

Board and batten paneling must be carefully installed and properly flashed so the back surfaces and edges remain dry. It also needs a protective topcoat of paint or stain to prevent deterioration from moisture or sunlight. As the panels age, it's common for the laminated layers to begin to separate. But, when the sheets eventually wear out, they're easy to replace.

You can also achieve the board and batten look by attaching narrow strips of wood, such as 1 × 2, vertically over seams between sheets of textured paneling, and also at regular intervals in the field area of the panels.

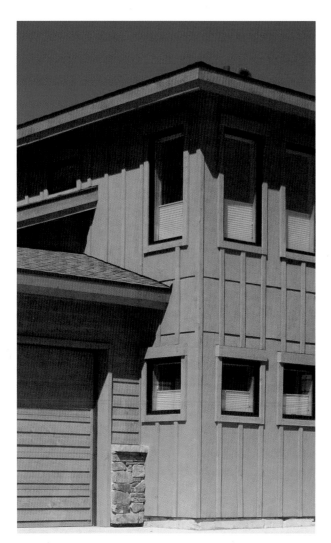

Board and batten siding was traditionally made up of wide, solid wood boards attached in a vertical configuration with narrow wood strips attached to conceal the gaps between boards. Today, this look is frequently recreated with plywood panels.

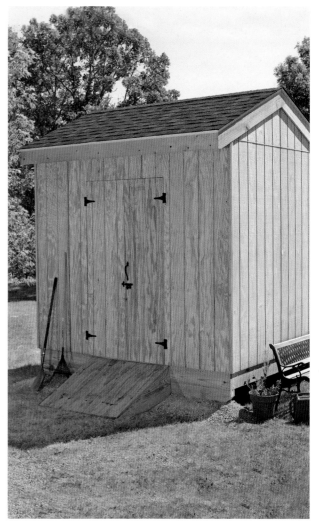

T1-11 paneling approximates the look of traditional board and batten siding, it is easy to install, and it is inexpensive. This paneling is still used for home siding, but you'll see it more often on sheds and outbuildings these days.

Log Cabin Siding

Log cabin siding is yet another wood siding alternative. Typically, white pine or cedar logs are stripped of bark, and then sawed into thin lengths of siding with the curvature of the log's surface left intact. The curvature can also be created at the mill by machines. The siding is installed with nails over building felt or housewrap, just like other siding options. The results are surprisingly convincing. It takes close inspection to realize that walls aren't made of whole logs. Any competent do-it-yourselfer can successfully install log cabin siding with common hand and power tools, and repairs are easy to make. Log cabin siding needs a top coat like other wood siding options to extend its serviceable life. Of course, log siding is also prone to degradation from insects, other animal pests, and rot. It's priced comparably to wood shakes or shingles.

You don't have to be a lumberjack to live in a log cabin home. Here, the rustic look of hewn logs and interlocking log-tail corners belies the fact that it is actually wood siding installed with a hammer and nails. It's a perfect do-it-yourself invitation to alpine living.

Masonry, Stone & Stucco

Various cement-based products give you many more options for durable, long-lasting siding. You're probably already familiar with stucco, which is a mixture of Portland and masonry cements, sand, and water. Stucco is installed in successive coats over a base of felt and metal lath. It can be applied to either wood-sheathed or masonry walls. A variety of colorants can be added to the finish coat. Alternatively, stucco can be painted with specially formulated elastomeric paints. Texturing is also a common practice, offering a blended, more natural appearance.

When properly installed, stucco will last for decades with only an occasional restorative coat. It can crumble or crack as a house settles, but stucco generally proves to be a tough, low-maintenance exterior finish. It may be used to coat entire exterior walls or for limited areas in conjunction with other siding materials. Removing stucco or creating new openings for windows and so forth is possible but labor-intensive.

Bonding cement can also be used to cover exterior walls. Essentially, it is a blend of Portland cement, sand, and fiberglass combined with an acrylic fortifier to create a cementitious plaster. Bonding cement is often applied in a smooth layer to hide cinder block or brick foundation surfaces. Because it isn't enhanced with color or texture, it's used sparingly to detail other forms of siding.

Mortared-in-place natural stone or full bricks are other attractive siding treatments to consider. Both are heavy and may require reinforced walls. The costs of quarrying and transporting natural stone make it expensive, but it's hard to argue against its beauty. Natural stone can be used sparingly to enhance foundation walls or pillars. It is common to combine rock with other forms of siding to help limit costs.

Conventional bricks provide a rugged or refined elegance, depending on the style you choose. They are durable, immune to insect damage, and fireproof. Brick repairs are considerably difficult, and creating new openings for windows or doors can be labor-intensive. When installed correctly, stone and brick will last the lifetime of your home.

If you want the look of stone or brick on your house without the rigors of cutting and moving heavy materials, consider using manufactured stone and

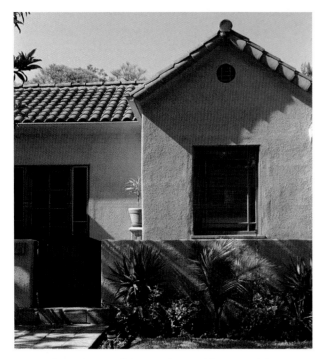

Stucco has a long tradition as a home siding material, especially in areas of the country where wood products are in scarce supply. It is a very durable siding material, but it does require some maintenance.

Brick veneer lends a stately appearance to ordinary-looking homes. It does help keep the elements out, but it does not have any structural value.

Stone veneer is a home design element that is on the rise in popularity. Today, more likely than not, the veneer you see is a lightweight, manufactured product rather than genuine stone.

Mortarless stone veneer siding is affixed to the facade of a house using only mechanical fasteners and supports. It provides the beauty of real masonry without the trouble of mixing and tooling mortar.

brick veneer. These products are made of cement that's cast into natural stone forms or brick shapes.

A multitude of simulated stone styles are available, including round, flat, textured, and smooth. Color options vary widely as well. Veneered stone is fixed in place with mortar over a base of felt and wire mesh. It weighs a fraction of real stone, is more affordable, and the end result is very convincing.

A mortarless system of brick veneer is often a better choice for do-it-yourselfers. Bricks simply stack in interlocking courses on the surface of a sheathed and wrapped wall. There is no mortar because every fourth course is fastened with screws to furring strips.

Even lap-style siding can be achieved using an innovative material composed of Portland cement, sand, and cellulose fiber formed into 12-foot planks

(called fiber cement). The siding is installed similarly to wood, vinyl, or metal lap siding using nails driven into wall framing. Fiber cement is relatively lightweight when compared to other cement-based siding products. It is reasonably flexible; will not rot, split, warp, or swell; offers good impact and water resistance; and is fireproof. Although color is not mixed in with siding planks, fiber cement is available primed or prepainted. It comes in various widths, thicknesses, and surface textures—including smooth, wood grain, and beaded.

Stucco, veneered stone, and mortarless brick can be installed with moderate masonry skills and some specialized tools. Fiber cement siding is also user-friendly, but you'll need electric shears and carbide blades on other tools. Hire a professional mason to install mortared, natural stone, or full brick.

Trim Materials

The trim system in your house draws from essentially the same pool of materials as siding: wood, vinyl, metal, or composites. Where possible, try and use like materials throughout.

Soffits can improve the appearance of open eave spaces by boxing these areas in. You can buy vented or unvented soffit panels to serve this purpose. If your home already has boxed-in soffits, you can retrofit them with round or continuous soffit vents, which are widely available at home centers. Venting soffit areas is a good way to prevent ice-damming problems in cold climates.

Gutter systems are essential for moving water off a roof and keeping foundations and walkways dry. You'll find a variety of vinyl and aluminum gutter components in the roofing section of any home center.

One drawback to installing a full system of these components is that you'll end up with many joints and seams that need to be sealed to prevent leaks. If you're in the market for a complete gutter replacement, you may want to consider having the work performed by a gutter installation company. They can fabricate gutter sections to any length on site using aluminum coil stock and an extrusion machine. This drastically reduces the number of seams in the system and creates a neater overall appearance.

If you live in a historical home, your gutters may be made of copper. Copper gutters are long lasting and can even be an attractive exterior detail, but most home centers do not carry replacement parts for them. Generally, you'll need to order these parts from a roofing supplier or Internet gutter supply source.

The parts of the trim package on your home include soffits (a) and fascia (b), corner trim (c), window trim (d), cornices (e), gable trim (not seen), vent covers (f), and gutters (g) with downspouts (h).

A low-maintenance track and panel kit made of aluminum or steel is an easy way to install a new soffit system with professional-looking results. Tracks and ventilated soffit segments are cut and fit with snap-together simplicity.

Gutter systems are available in vinyl, enameled steel and aluminum at any home center. The troughs and downspouts are sold in 10-ft. lengths, and the individual connectors, caps, and fittings are sold separately. Gutter systems made from other materials, such as copper, can be purchased from roof material suppliers and through the Internet.

Exterior trim pieces include both raw materials for making custom trim and prefabricated parts made from wood, wood composite, or molded plastics. Plastic or composite products typically come in white only, but many of them are paintable.

Estimating Roofing & Siding

Ordering Roofing Materials

Roofing materials are ordered in squares, with one square equaling 100 square feet. To determine how many squares are needed, first figure out the square footage of your roof. The easiest way to make this calculation is to multiply the length by the width of each section of roof, and then add the numbers together.

For steep roofs and those with complex designs, do your measuring from the ground and multiply by a number based on the slope of your roof. Measure the length and width of your house, include the overhangs, then multiply the numbers together to determine the overall square footage. Using the chart at the lower right, multiply the square footage by a number based on the roof's slope. Add 10 percent for waste, then divide the total square footage by 100 to determine the number of squares you need. Don't spend time calculating and subtracting the areas that won't be covered, such as skylights and chimneys. They're usually small enough that they don't impact the number of squares you need. Besides, it's good to have extra materials for waste, mistakes, and later repairs.

To determine how much flashing you'll need, measure the length of the valley to figure valley flashing, the lengths of the eaves and rakes to figure drip edge, and the number and size of vent pipes to figure vent flashing.

Asphalt shingles come in packaged bundles weighing around 65 pounds each. For typical three-tab shingles, three bundles will cover one square (100 sq. ft.) of roof.

Calculate the roof's surface by multiplying the height of the roof by the width. Do this for each section, then add the totals together. Divide that number by 100, add 10 percent for waste, and that's the number of squares of roofing materials you need.

Conversion Chart

Slope	Multiply by	Slope	Multiply by
2 in 12	1.02	8 in 12	1.20
3 in 12	1.03	9 in 12	1.25
4 in 12	1.06	10 in 12	1.30
5 in 12	1.08	11 in 12	1.36
6 in 12	1.12	12 in 12	1.41
7 in 12	1.16		

Ordering Siding Materials

Siding is sold by the linear foot, square foot, board foot, or square, depending on the type of material. To determine the amount of siding materials you'll need, calculate the square footage of each wall, then add them together to get your total surface area.

To figure the square footage for a wall, multiply the length of the wall by the height. Calculate the area on the gable end of a wall by using the formula for triangles, which is one-half the length of the base multiplied by the height of the triangle. You won't need to subtract for areas covered by windows and doors, and you won't need to add an extra 10 percent for waste. The window and door areas are roughly equal to the amount of waste you'll need.

Use your height and length measurements from the walls to determine how many feet of starter strip, channels, corner posts, and trim you'll need. Keep in mind you'll probably also need to apply trim or channels around all of your doors and windows.

Depending on the siding material you're ordering, you may need extra material to allow for overlap. For example, if you want to install 10" lap siding with an 8" exposure, you'll need to account for a 2" overlap for each board. Likewise, the exposure rate for wood shakes or shingles will determine how many squares you'll need. Depending on the exposure rate, one square of shingles could cover 80 sq. ft, 100 sq. ft, or even 120 sq. ft. Most manufacturers have charts that show how much material is needed to cover a specified number of square feet at various rates of exposure. If you have trouble estimating how much material you need to purchase, ask your supplier for help.

Estimate the amount of siding you'll need by calculating the square footage of each wall, then adding the numbers together. To determine the square footage of a wall, multiply the wall length by its height. Subtract the square footage of all windows and doors, and then add 10 percent for waste to get square footage. Don't forget about corner trim, J-channel and other trim pieces.

Working Safely

Working on the exterior of a house presents challenges not faced in the interior, such as dealing with the weather, working at heights, and staying clear of power lines. By taking a few commonsense safety precautions, you can perform exterior work safely.

Dress appropriately for the job and weather. Avoid working in extreme temperatures, hot or cold, and never work outdoors during a storm or high winds.

Work with a helper whenever possible—especially when working at heights. If you must work alone, tell a family member or friend so the person can check in with you periodically. Keep you cell phone handy at all times.

Don't use tools or work at heights after consuming alcohol. If you're taking medications, read the label and follow the recommendations regarding the use of tools and equipment.

When using ladders, extend the top of the ladder 3 feet above the roof edge for greater stability. Climb on and off the ladder at a point as close to the ground as possible. Use caution and keep your center of gravity low when moving from a ladder onto a roof. Keep your hips between the side rails when reaching over the side of a ladder, and be careful not to extend yourself too far or it could throw off your balance. Move the ladder as often as necessary to avoid overreaching. Finally, don't exceed the workload rating for your ladder. Read and follow the load limits and safety instructions listed on the label.

Wear appropriate clothing and safety equipment whenever working high above ground. Eye protection and hearing protection are very important when using power tools or pneumatic tools. And if you'll be climbing on a roof, wear tennis shoes or any sturdy shoe with a soft sole designed for gripping. When roofing, always avoid hard-soled shoes or boots, which can damage shingles and are prone to slipping.

Use a GFCI extension cord when working outdoors. GFCIs (ground-fault circuit-interrupters) shut off power if a short circuit occurs.

Use cordless tools to eliminate the hazards of extension cords, especially when working from ladders.

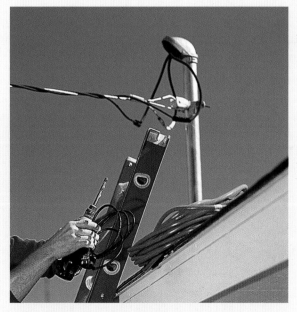

Use fiberglass or wood ladders when working near power cables. Exercise extreme caution around these cables, and only work near them when absolutely necessary.

Never climb a ladder with a loaded air nailer attached to a pressurized air hose. Even with trigger safeties, air guns pose a serious danger to the operator as well as anyone who may be standing near the ladder.

Fall-Arresting Gear

Even if you consider yourself dexterous and are comfortable working in high places, all it takes is one misstep on a roof to lead to a tragic fall. Despite the fact that many professional roofers never don safety harnesses, you should seriously consider investing in personal fall-arresting gear if you plan to reroof your home. Fall-arresting gear consists of several components. You wear a webbed body harness that spreads the impact of a fall over your shoulders, thighs, and back to reduce injury. Harnesses are made to fit average adult builds. The harness connects to a shock absorber and a lanyard around 6 feet in length. A self-locking, rope-grab mechanism attaches the lanyard to a lifeline that must be fastened securely to a ridge anchor screwed to roof framing. In the event that you slip or fall, the rope grab will limit your fall to the length of the lanyard because it will not move down the lifeline unless you override the locking mechanism by hand.

Most rental centers will not carry fall-arresting gear, and a complete system will cost several hundred dollars. When compared with the loss of life or limb, however, your real investment is small. Better yet, you'll have it available any time you need to get on the roof for cleaning tasks or to make repairs.

Tools & Materials ▸

Pry bar
Drill/driver
Harness
Lanyard

Rope grab
Synthetic fiber lifeline
Ridge anchor

Personal fall-arresting gear consists of a lifeline (A) with mechanical rope grab (B) and lanyard (C); a metal ridge anchor (D); and a body harness (E).

A metal ridge anchor must be secured with screws to the roof framing. Follow the manufacturer's recommendations for proper screw sizing, and make sure your attachment points go beyond the roof sheathing into the roof trusses or rafters.

The rope-grab mechanism allows you to move up a roof along the lifeline without interference. To move down the roof, you'll need to override the grab by hand. As soon as you release it, the lock engages again.

Lifting & Staging Shingles

Carrying bundles of asphalt shingles up a ladder and onto a roof deck is a grueling job, especially if you have as many as 50 bundles to haul. With each bundle weighing 65 to 75 pounds, you need to be concerned about two issues: your safety and how to stage the material for efficient installation. The easiest solution is to simply have your roofing supplier unload the shingles directly to your roof with a boom truck or conveyor belt. This will cost a nominal fee, but the physical exertion you'll avoid may be well worth the cost.

If you must manually unload the bundles from your supplier while on the roof, place the first bundle or two flat on the roof to serve as a base, then stack subsequent bundles partially on the first two and partially on the roof deck. Limit your stack sizes to a dozen bundles or less to help distribute the weight. If possible, place the bundles at a point where two roofs intersect for added stability. Distribute your stacks evenly along the length of the roof ridge so they are readily available wherever you're working as the job progresses. Since the ridge is the last area shingled, most of your supply should be used and out of the way by the time you reach the peak.

For smaller jobs, you may elect to simply carry the bundles up to the roof yourself. In this situation, wear a back support brace to prevent back strain, and carry one bundle at a time over your shoulder so you can keep one hand on a ladder rung at all times. Hand off each bundle to a helper waiting for you on the roof. Switch jobs before you get tired to conserve your energy and share the really hard work.

How to Stage Shingles

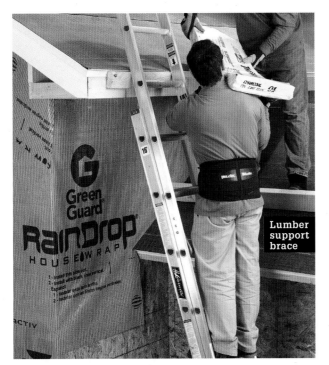

When you must carry bundles up a ladder, wear a lumbar support brace to prevent back strain. Take your time carrying each bundle, and rest often. Make sure the bundle is well balanced before you ascend the ladder. If you feel the weight of the bundle start to shift, drop the bundle immediately for your safety. Have a helper waiting for you when you reach the roof deck so you don't have to unload bundles near the eave or risk a fall.

Build stable stacks of a dozen bundles of shingles near the roof ridge. Create stacks by placing two bundles flat on the roof, then adding more bundles that straddle both the first two and the roof deck. When possible, stack bundles where two roof areas meet.

Use plywood blocking to level and stabilize the legs of the scaffolding or ladder. If the scaffolding has wheels, lock them securely with the hand brakes.

Use an extension ladder when making quick repairs to gutters, fascia, and soffits, and for gaining access to roofs.

Stabilize your ladder with stakes driven into the ground, behind each ladder foot. Install sturdy blocking under the legs of the ladder if the ground is uneven.

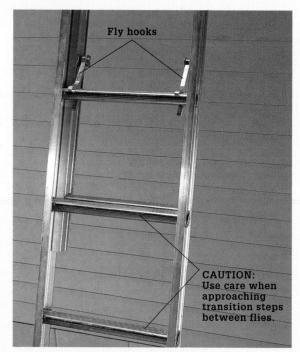

Fly hooks

CAUTION: Use care when approaching transition steps between flies.

Make sure both fly hooks are secure before climbing an extension ladder. The open ends of the hooks should grip a rung on the lower fly extension.

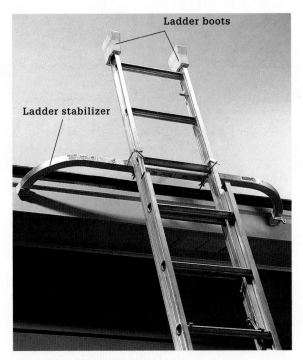

Ladder boots

Ladder stabilizer

Attach an adjustable ladder stabilizer to your ladder to minimize the chance of slipping. Rest the feet of the stabilizer against broad, flat, stable surfaces.

Anchor an extension ladder by tying the top to a secure area, such as a chimney, or a securely mounted screw eye.

Attach a ladder jack to your ladder by slipping the rung mounts over the ladder rungs. Level the platform body arm, and lock it into place.

Set the plank in place on the platform arm. Adjust the arm's end stop to hold the plank in place.

Setting Up Scaffolding

A set of ladders and roof jacks may be all the support you need for roofing projects, but replacing siding higher than the first floor of your home will require some type of platform-style scaffolding. It isn't safe to slide a plank between two ladders and call it good; the setup lacks stability and protection from swaying. A broad platform is more helpful for staging materials and tools and moving around freely.

Steel tubular scaffolding is available from any rental center for daily, weekly, or monthly rates. It should come with a complete set of instructions for how to assemble the pieces correctly. Begin by setting up the scaffolding on flat ground, free from mud and construction debris. If you have to adjust the first level for uneven terrain, follow the instructions carefully. Do not use stacks of boards or cinder blocks to create a level surface.

Each stage of scaffolding consists of two end frames, several crossbraces, and planking that makes up the platform. Set up the first level of scaffolding on steel base plates, if your equipment has them, or on wide wood base supports. Use string lines and bubble levels to make sure the end frames are level and plumb. If the scaffolding has screw jack adjusters, use them to level the structure.

Make sure all the components are fully seated in their joints, then add the planking to create the first platform. The platform shouldn't sway. Platform planks should line up evenly to prevent tripping hazards. Keep gaps between the planks to 1 inch or less. Once the first level of staging is secure, repeat the process to build the second stage of scaffold. Make sure any connective locking pins are securely engaged from one stage to the next. If you need to build scaffolding more than 16 feet high, use wall brackets that clamp to the scaffold and bolt them into solid wall framing for added stability. No matter how high your scaffold becomes, it must remain as stable as the first stage. Add any guard rails, end rails, or toe boards that may be required.

Renting scaffolding is an excellent investment if you are painting or installing siding. You easily recoup the cost in time savings and safety.

Tools & Materials ▶

Scaffolding components
String line
Levels
Shovel
(for leveling the installation area)

Securing Scaffolding ▶

Sections of scaffolding are connected with locking cotter pins that fit through holes aligned in the tubular legs. The cotter pins feature clips that snap around both ends to keep them from slipping out of the tubular legs. Even with these locking pins it's always a good idea to test the connections daily before using your scaffolding.

How to Set Up Scaffolding

1

Clear the setup area of debris, and then assemble the first two end frames and crossbraces to create the bottom stage of scaffold framing.

2

Use string lines and levels to check end frames for level and plumb. Adjust the structure using screw jacks mounted to the frame legs, or by a leveling technique recommended by the manufacturer. The end-frame legs should rest firmly on wood or steel base plates. Never use stacks of boards or cinder blocks for leveling purposes. Lay the planks in position to form the bottom platform.

3

Assemble the parts for the second stage on top of the first stage. Make sure all joints and connective locking pins are fully engaged from one stage to the next (see tip, previous page).

4

For extreme heights that require more than two stages, you need to secure the scaffolding to the house with chains or wall tie-in brackets that clamp to the scaffolding. Make sure to fasten to wall framing—not to sheathing only.

Pump-Jack Scaffolding

Now and then you may see professional siding crews using an alternative form of scaffolding called pump-jack scaffolding. Pump jacks consist of long wood or aluminum support posts that extend from the ground to the roof line. A foot-operated jack mounts on each pole and supports wooden or aluminum walk planks. Some designs also include a secondary platform that can be used as a workbench or serve as a guardrail. The advantage to using pump jacks over staged scaffolding is adjustability. By pumping the foot lever on each mounting post, workers can raise the platform in 6-inch intervals. Pump jacks are particularly well suited for siding and painting projects, which require moving up the walls incrementally. Staged scaffolding offers a larger platform, but it's set at a fixed height.

Pump jacks are less common than staged scaffolding at rental centers. Siding contractors lend them out during the off-season as well. With some research, you can find them for $150 a pair. While pump jacks are stable and versatile, they don't offer the same level of fall protection as a full framework of scaffolding, and you won't have a great deal of room to place extra project materials and tools. If you have access to fall-arresting gear, wear it.

Tools & Materials ▸

Hammer	Wood support posts
16d nails	(if applicable)
Pump jack	Fall-arresting gear
components	(highly recommended)

Pump jacks are a convenient alternative to scaffolding. They offer greater foot space and hence are safer than ladders. The steel jacks that support a cross-plank are raised and lowered on a pole or post by foot operation.

How to Use Pump-Jack Scaffolding

Assemble the components. You'll need a pair of foot-operated pumps that raise a work platform along wood or aluminum poles. The components assemble quickly and provide more flexibility than standard scaffolding for working at varying heights. They're ideal for siding installation.

Build the support posts. Depending on the pump jacks you use, you may need to first build the posts from common 2 × 4s and 16d nails. Wood posts can be made up to 30 ft. tall, provided the joints are staggered and mending plates are nailed over every joint.

Secure the posts to the framing members of the exterior wall using triangular pump jack post brackets.

Install the platform and adjust the height as needed. Two operators can raise or lower the work platform quickly, but only one person can operate one pump at a time. Plan your material quantities and tool requirements carefully before raising the platform. Space is more restricted on the platform, so it must be lowered down to replenish tools and materials.

Installing Roof Jacks

Sure footing isn't an issue when you're working on a low-pitched roof, but it becomes a real safety concern for roofs with 7-in-12 or steeper pitches. In these situations, you need to install roof jacks to create a stable work area and navigate the roof safely. Roof jacks are steel braces that nail temporarily to roof decking to support a 2 × 8 or 2 × 10 perch. In addition to improving your footing, roof jacks also provide a flatter surface to stand on, which can help reduce ankle strain. Roof jacks should be installed every 4 feet of plank length with 16d nails. They're inexpensive and available wherever roofing products are sold.

Tools & Materials ▸

Pry bar
Hammer
16d nails
Roof jacks
2 × 8 or 2 × 10 lumber

Roof jacks are steel braces that you nail to the roof deck. Installed in pairs, they support a dimensional board (usually a 2 × 8) to create a sturdy work platform on a sloped roof.

How to Install Roof Jacks

Nail roof jacks to the roof at the fourth or fifth course. Drive 16d nails into the overlap, or dead area, where they won't be exposed. Install one jack every 4 ft., with a 6" to 12" overhang at the ends of the boards.

Shingle over the tops of the roof jacks. Rest a 2 × 8 or 2 × 10 board on the jacks. Fasten the board with a nail driven through the hole in the lip of each roof jack.

When the project is complete, remove the boards and jacks. Position the end of a flat pry bar over each nail and drive in the nail by rapping the shank with a hammer.

Preparing the Job Site

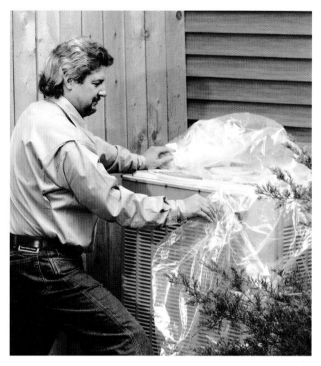

Cover external air conditioning units, appliances, and other structures near the house. Make sure the power is turned off before covering them, and don't use them while they're covered.

Remove exterior shutters and decorative trim to protect them from damage and make it easier to paint.

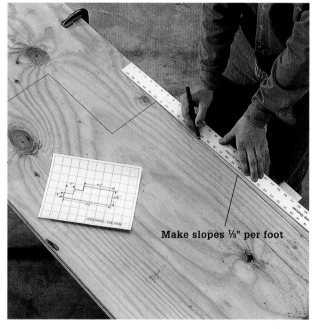

Make slopes ⅛" per foot

Transfer the measurements for the side forms from your working sketch onto ¾" exterior-grade plywood. Cut out the forms along the cutting lines, using a jigsaw. Save time by clamping two pieces of plywood together and cutting both side forms at the same time. Add a ⅛" per foot, back-to-front slope to the landing part of the form.

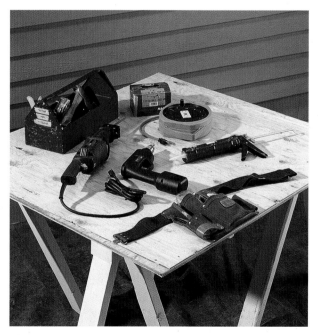

Create a tool platform with sawhorses and a piece of plywood. Tools spread on the ground are a safety hazard and moisture can damage them. It's safer and more efficient to organize your tools so they're dry and easy to find.

Installing Roofing

Whether you plan to remove all the old shingles on your roof and replace them, shingle over the existing layer, or simply make some necessary repairs to a few shingles or leaky valley flashing, your primary goal in any roofing project is to make the roof watertight. All other considerations are secondary to moving water off the roof and keeping it out of your home's interior.

Without a clear understanding of how to install underlayment, flashings, and shingles properly, a leak is not only possible but probably unavoidable. The good news is that installing roofing materials correctly isn't difficult to learn, and this chapter will show you how. Asphalt shingles, wood shakes, or shingles and EPDM membrane roofing make excellent do-it-yourself projects. You not only save the money you would have paid a professional roofer to do the job, but you also have the satisfaction of knowing you did the job well. The boasting rights will be all yours.

In this chapter:

Anatomy of a Roof

The elements of a roof system work together to provide shelter, drainage, and ventilation. The roof covering is composed of sheathing, felt paper, and shingles. Metal flashing is attached in valleys and around chimneys, vent pipes, and other roof elements to seal out water. Soffits cover and protect the eaves area below the roof overhang. Fascia, usually attached at the ends of the rafters, supports soffit panels as well as a gutter and downspout system. Soffit vents and roof vents keep fresh air circulating throughout the roof system.

Roof vents

Vent pipe

Rake edge

Roof sheathing

Fascia

Valley flashing

Chimney cap

Counter flashing

Ridge

Shingles

Base flashing

Soffit vents

Soffit panel

Valley

Eave

Gutters

Tools & Materials

Working conditions on a roof can be arduous, so make the job as easy as possible by gathering the right tools and equipment before you begin.

Some of these tools, such as a pneumatic nailer and roofer's hatchet, are specific to roofing projects. If you don't have them and don't want to buy them, you can rent them from a rental center.

Specialty roofing tools include roof jacks (A) for use on steep roofs (page 58), roofing shovel (B) for tearoff work, pneumatic nailer (C), utility knife with hooked blade (D) for trimming shingles, roofing hammer with alignment guides and hatchet blade (E) for shingle installation, and a release magnet for site cleanup (F).

Use roof jacks on steep roofs. Nail the supports at the fourth or fifth course of shingles, and add the widest board the supports will hold.

For more secure footing, fashion a roofing ladder by nailing wood strips across a pair of 2 × 4s. Secure the ladder to the roof jacks, and use it to maintain your footing.

Drip edge

Preformed valley flashing

Rolled flashing material

Aviation snips

Vent pipe flashing

Step flashing blanks

Skylight flashing kit (partial)

Roof flashing can be hand cut or purchased in preformed shapes and sizes. Long pieces of valley flashing, base flashing, top saddles, and other nonstandard pieces can be cut from rolled flashing material using aviation snips. Step flashing blanks can be bought in standard sizes and bent to fit. Drip edge and vent pipe flashing are available preformed. Skylight flashing usually comes as a kit with the window. Complicated flashings, such as chimney crickets, can be custom fabricated by a metalworker.

Aluminum roofing nails

Rubber gasket nails

Galvanized roofing nails

Roofing nail coil (for pneumatic nailer)

Different fasteners are specially developed for different jobs. Use galvanized roofing nails to hand nail shingles; use aluminum nails for aluminum flashing; use rubber gasket nails for galvanized metal flashing; and use nail coils for pneumatic nailers.

Felt paper (30#)

Roofing cement

Ice-guard membrane

Common roofing materials include 30# felt paper for use as underlayment; ice-guard membrane for use as underlayment in cold climates; and tubes of roofing cement for sealing small holes, cracks, and joints.

Completing the Tear Off

Removing shingles, commonly referred to in the roofing trade as the tear off, can be done rather quickly. This makes it one of the more satisfying parts of a reshingling project. If you can't reshingle your entire roof in one day, tear off one section of roofing at a time, roof that section, then move on to the next part of the roof.

The tear off produces a lot of debris and waste. A few preparatory steps make cleanup much easier (see page 59). Lay tarps on the ground and lean sheets of plywood against the house to protect shrubbery and the siding.

If renting a dumpster isn't practical, set wheelbarrows on tarps as an alternative for catching debris. However, you'll still be responsible for disposing of the old roof, which will probably require several trips to the landfill. To work efficiently, have another person deal with the debris on the ground as you work on the roof.

Tools & Materials ▸

Hammer	Rake
Chisel	Tin snips
Pry bar	Reciprocating saw
Utility knife	Drill
Roofing shovel or pitchfork	Protective gear
	Tarps
Broom	Wheelbarrow or
Release magnet	Dumpster

Rent a dumpster from a waste disposal company or your local waste management department. If you are re-roofing, position the dumpster directly below the roof edge, so when you're tearing off the old roofing materials, the debris can be dumped from the roof directly into the dumpster.

How to Tear Off Old Shingles

Remove the ridge cap using a flat pry bar. Pry up the cap shingles at the nail locations.

Working downward from the peak, tear off the felt paper and old shingles with a roofing shovel or pitchfork.

Unless flashing is in exceptional condition, remove it by slicing through the roofing cement that attaches it to the shingles. You may be able to salvage flashing pieces, such as chimney saddles and crickets, and reuse them.

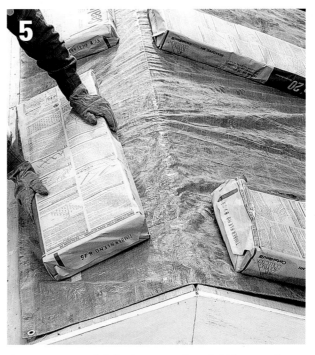

After removing the shingles, felt paper, and flashing from the entire tear-off section, pry out any remaining nails and sweep the roof with a broom.

If an unexpected delay keeps you from finishing a section before nightfall, cover any unshingled sections using tarps weighted down with shingle bundles.

Replacing Sheathing

Once the tear off is complete, inspect the roof decking for damage. If there are any soft spots on the roof, or if a portion of the sheathing is damaged, it'll need to be replaced. Most older roofs are constructed with board sheathing, usually 1 × 6s, while newer roofs typically use 4 × 8-ft. sheets of plywood or oriented strandboard (OSB). Even if your roof has board sheathing, you can make the repairs with plywood, as we're doing here. Make sure the plywood is the same thickness as your current sheathing and rated for exterior use.

Before cutting into your roof, check under the sheathing for wires. There may be telephone wires or television cable hidden in the roof, and you don't want to cut through them. Avoid walking on the damaged sheathing. If you have access from the underside, it may be safer to remove the sheathing from below.

Damage to the roof sheathing normally occurs because there is a violation of the roof seal, typically occurring around a chimney, roof vent, skylight or another flashed object. If you will be reflashing the roof make sure you don't repeat any mistakes. If you are making only localized repairs, be sure that you identify and correct the source of the moisture that's caused the deterioration. If the damage is located near the eave and is not caused by a flashing problem or a leak in the roof covering, it is probably caused by an ice dam (see page 234).

Tools & Materials ▸

Circular saw	Sheathing
Reciprocating saw	2 × 4 nailing strips
Tape measure	3", 2¼" deck screws
Chalk line	Plywood
Flat pry bar	8d ring-shank
Drill	siding nails

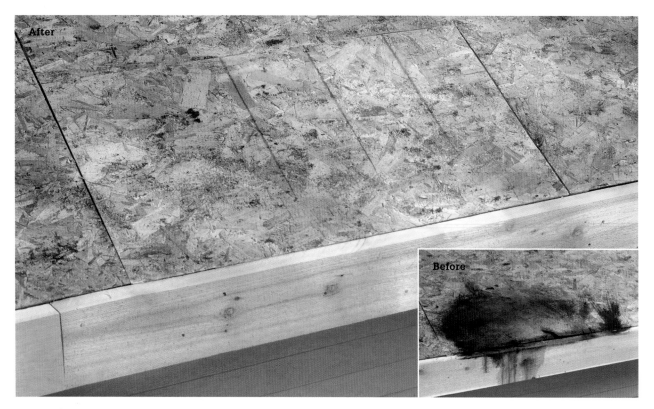

After

Before

Inspect for damaged sheathing after tear off is completed. Replace damaged roof deck, making sure the new seams fall over rafters. Also replace trim boards in the repair area if they have become damaged.

How to Replace Damaged Sheathing

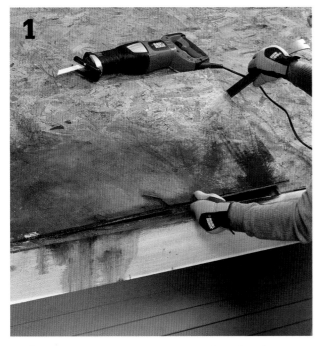

Use a reciprocating saw to cut next to the rafters in an area that extends well beyond the damaged area. Pry out the damaged sections using a pry bar.

Attach 2 × 4 nailing strips to the inside edges of the rafters using 3" deck screws

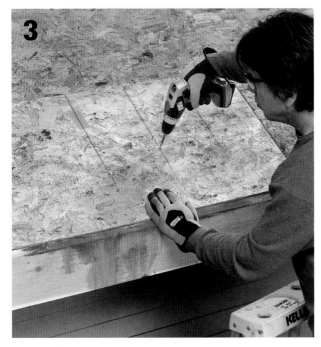

Use exterior grade plywood to make a patch. Measure the cutout area, allow for a ⅛" gap on all sides for expansion, and cut the patch to size. Attach the patch to the rafters and nailing strips using 2¼" deck screws or 8d ring-shank siding nails.

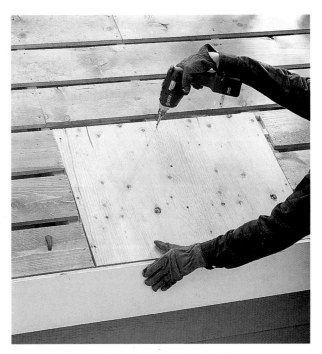

Option: If your existing roof deck is made of boards (1 × 6 was common before plywood took over the market), it is perfectly acceptable to use plywood when replacing a section of the deck. The plywood should be the same thickness as the boards, generally, ¾".

Underlayment

Felt paper, also called building paper, is installed on roof decks as insurance in case leaks develop in shingles or flashing. It's sold in several weights, but heavier 30# paper is a good choice for use under shingles, and may be required by code.

In cold climates, codes often require an additional underlayment called "ice and water shield" or "ice guard" that's used instead of standard felt paper for the first one or two courses of underlayment, which is what we're showing here. In cold climates, apply as many courses of ice and water shield as it takes to cover 24 inches past the roof overhang. An adhesive membrane, the ice guard bonds with the roof sheathing to create a barrier against water backing up from ice dams.

If you apply the felt paper straight, you can use the lines on the paper as references when installing the roofing materials. This will help keep your rows of shingles running in a straight line.

Tools & Materials ▶

Chalk line	Caulk gun
Hammer stapler	30# felt paper
Flat pry bar	Ice and water shield
Utility knife	Staples
Tape measure	Roofing cement

For optimum roof protection, apply ice and water shield in valleys, along the eaves, and along the rake edges of the roof. Apply 30# felt paper over the remainder of the roof.

How to Install Underlayment

Snap a chalk line 35⅝" up from the eaves, so the first course of the 36"-wide membrane will overhang the eaves by ⅜". Install a course of ice and water shield, using the chalk line as a reference, and peeling back the protective backing as you unroll it.

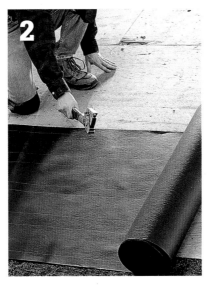

Measuring up from the eaves, make a mark 32" above the top of the last row of underlayment, and snap another chalk line. Roll out the next course of felt paper (or ice guard, if required) along the chalk line, overlapping the first course by 4". *Tip: Drive staples every 6 to 12" along the edges of felt paper, and one staple per sq. ft. in the field area.*

At valleys, roll felt paper across from both sides, overlapping the ends by 36". Install felt paper up to the ridge—ruled side up—snapping horizontal lines every two or three rows to check alignment. Overlap horizontal seams by 4", vertical seams by 12", and hips and ridges by 6". Trim the courses flush with the rake edges.

Apply felt paper up to an obstruction, then resume laying the course on the opposite side (make sure to maintain the line). Cut a patch that overlaps the felt paper by 12" on all sides. Make a crosshatch cutout for the obstruction. Position the patch over the obstruction, staple it in place, then caulk the seams with roofing cement.

At the bottom of dormers and sidewalls, tuck the felt paper under the siding where it intersects with the roof. Carefully pry up the siding and tuck at least 2" of paper under it. Also tuck the paper under counter flashing or siding on chimneys and skylights. Leave the siding or counter flashing or siding unfastened until after you install the step flashing.

Drip Edge

Drip edge is a flashing that's installed along the eaves and rake edges of the roof to direct water away from the roof decking. Although its job is to deflect water, it also gives the edges of the roof an attractive finish. A corrosion-resistant material, drip edge won't stain your roofing materials or fascia.

The flashing is installed along the eaves before the felt paper is attached to allow water to run off the roof in the event it gets under the shingles. Drip edge is installed at the rake edges after the felt paper has been attached to keep wind-driven rain from getting under the paper.

Drip edge is always nailed directly to the roof decking, rather than to the fascia or rake boards. The nail heads are later covered by roofing materials.

There are two basic styles of drip edge. One is the C-style drip edge that doesn't have an overhang, and the other, much more common, type is the extended-profile drip edge that has a hemmed overhang along the edges.

Tools & Materials ▸

Hammer	Roofing nails
Tape measure	Circular saw
Aviation snips	30# felt paper
Drip edge	Ice and water shield

Drip edge

Drip edge flashing prevents water from working its way under the roofing materials along the eaves and rake edges of the roof.

How to Install Drip Edge

Cut a 45° miter at one end of the drip edge using aviation snips. Place the drip edge along the eaves end of the roof, aligning the mitered end with the rake edge. Nail the drip edge in place every 12".

Overlap pieces of drip edge by 2". Install drip edge across the entire eaves, ending with a mitered cut on the opposite corner.

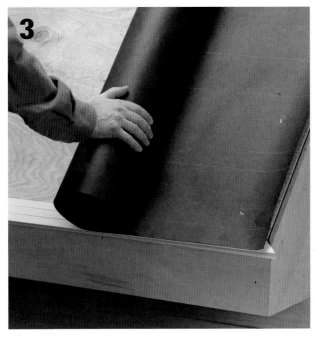

Apply felt paper, and ice guard if needed, to the roof, overhanging the eaves by ⅜" (see pages 70 to 71).

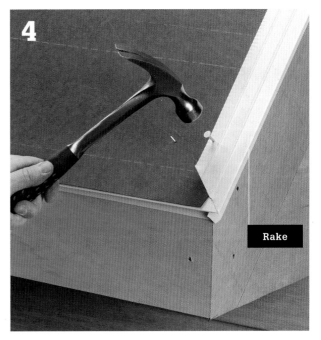

Cut a 45° miter in a piece of drip edge and install it along the rake edge, forming a miter joint with the drip edge along the eaves. Overlap pieces by 2", making sure the higher piece is on top at the overlap. Apply drip edge all the way to the peak. Install drip edge along the other rake edges the same way.

Flashing

Flashing is a metal or rubber barrier used to protect the seams around roof elements or between adjoining roof surfaces. Metal flashings are made of either galvanized steel, copper, or aluminum. Whatever metal you choose, use nails made of the same material. Mixing metals can cause corrosion and discoloration.

Flashing's primary job is to channel water off the roof and away from seams. It's installed in areas where shingles can't be applied and would otherwise be prone to leaks. Some flashing, such as the valley flashing shown on the opposite page, is installed over the underlayment, prior to the installation of the shingles. Other flashing, such as flashing for vent pipes, is installed in conjunction with the shingles, and is shown as part of the roofing sequences throughout this chapter.

While most flashing is preformed, you'll sometimes need to bend your own. This is especially true for flashing around roof elements, such as chimneys and dormers, that often need to be custom fit. Building a bending jig, as shown on the opposite page, allows you to easily bend flashing to fit your needs.

When installing flashing around roof elements, the flashing should be secured to one surface only—usually the roof deck. Use only roofing cement to bond the flashing to the roof elements. The flashing must be able to flex as the roof element and the roof deck expand and contract. If the flashing is fastened to both the roof deck and roof element, it will tear or loosen.

Tools & Materials ▸

Aviation snips	Galvanized metal
Caulk gun	valley flashing
Flat pry bar	Roofing cement
Roofing hammer	Roofing nails or
Tape measure	rubber gasket nails
Trowel	Scrap wood
Clamp	Screws

Flashing is a critical component of roofs that helps keep the structure watertight. Most roofs have flashing in the valleys and around dormers. This roof uses several valley flashings as well as flashing around the window and around the bump-out in the roof.

How to Bend Flashing

To bend flashing, make a bending jig by driving screws into a piece of wood, creating a space one-half the width of the flashing when measured from the edge of the board. Clamp the bending jig to a work surface. Lay a piece of flashing flat on the board and bend it over the edge.

Use the old flashing as a template for making replacement pieces. This is especially useful for reproducing complicated flashing, such as saddle flashing for chimneys and dormers.

How to Install Valley Flashing

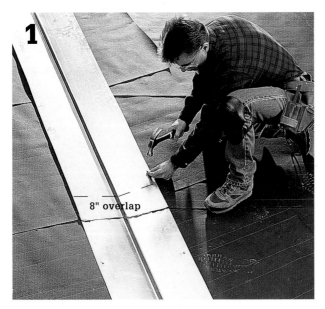

8" overlap

Starting at the eaves, set a piece of valley flashing into the valley so the bottom of the V rests in the crease of the valley. Nail the flashing at 12" intervals along each side. Trim the end of the flashing at the eaves so it's flush with the drip edge at each side. Working toward the top of the valley, add flashing pieces so they overlap by at least 8" until you reach the ridge.

Spine

Let the top edge of the flashing extend a few inches beyond the ridge. Bend the flashing over the ridge so it lies flat on the opposite side of the roof. If you're installing preformed flashing, make a small cut in the spine for easier bending. Cover nail heads with roofing cement (unless you're using rubber gasket nails). Apply roofing cement along the side edges of the flashing.

Asphalt Shingles

If you want to install asphalt shingles on your roof, then you're in good company. Asphalt shingles, also known as composition shingles, are the roofing of choice for nearly four out of five homeowners in America. They perform well in all types of climate, are available in a multitude of colors, shapes, and textures to complement every housing design, and are less expensive than most other roofing products.

Asphalt shingles are available as either fiberglass shingles or organic shingles. Both types are made with asphalt, the difference being that one uses a fiberglass reinforcing mat, while the other uses a cellulose-fiber mat. Fiberglass shingles are lighter, thinner, and have a better fire rating. Organic shingles have a higher tear strength, are more flexible in cold climates, and are used more often in northern regions.

Although the roofing market has exploded with innovative new asphalt shingle designs, such as the architectural or laminated shingle that offers a three-dimensional look, the standard three-tab asphalt shingle is still the most common, which is the project we're featuring here. The tabs provide an easy reference for aligning shingles for installation.

To help the job get done faster, rent an air compressor and pneumatic roofing gun. This will greatly reduce the time you spend nailing.

Tools & Materials ▸

Aviation snips	Chalk gun
Carpenter's square	Flashing
Chalk line	Shingles
Flat bar	Nailing cartridges
Roofer's hatchet or	Roofing cement
pneumatic nailer	Roofing nails
Utility knife	(7/8", 1¼")
Straightedge	Rubber gasket nails
Tape measure	

Stagger shingles for effective protection against leaks. If the tab slots are aligned in successive rows, water forms channels, increasing erosion of the mineral surface of the shingles. Creating a 6" offset between rows of shingles—with the three-tab shingles shown above—ensures that the tab slots do not align.

How to Install Three-tab Shingles

Cover the roof with felt paper (pages 70 to 71) and install drip edge (pages 72 to 73). Snap a chalk line onto the felt paper or ice guard 11½" up from the eaves edge, to mark the alignment of the starter course. This will result in a ½" shingle overhang for standard 12" shingles. *Tip: Use blue chalk rather than red. Red chalk will stain roofing materials.*

Trim off one-half (6") of an end tab on a shingle. Position the shingle upside down, so the tabs are aligned with the chalk line and the half-tab is flush against the rake edge. Drive ⅞" roofing nails near each end, 1" down from each slot between tabs. Butt a full upside-down shingle next to the trimmed shingle, and nail it. Fill out the row, trimming the last shingle flush with the opposite rake edge.

Apply the first full course of shingles over the starter course with the tabs pointing down. Begin at the rake edge where you began the starter row. Place the first shingle so it overhangs the rake edge by ⅜" and the eaves edge by ½". Make sure the top of each shingle is flush with the top of the starter course, following the chalk line.

Snap a chalk line from the eaves edge to the ridge to create a vertical line to align the shingles. Choose an area with no obstructions, as close as possible to the center of the roof. The chalk line should pass through a slot or a shingle edge on the first full shingle course. Use a carpenter's square to establish a line perpendicular to the eaves edge.

(continued)

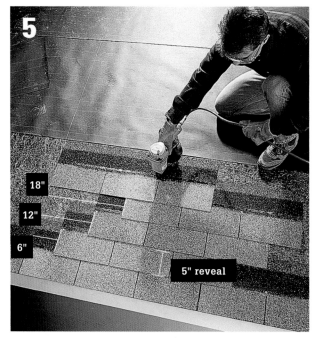

Use the vertical reference line to establish a shingle pattern with slots that are offset by 6" in succeeding courses. Tack down a shingle 6" to one side of the vertical line, 5" above the bottom edge of the first-course shingles to start the second row. Tack down shingles for the third and fourth courses, 12" and 18" from the vertical line. Butt the fifth course against the line.

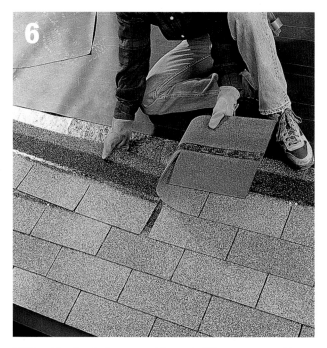

Fill in shingles in the second through fifth courses, working upward from the second course and maintaining a consistent 5" reveal. Slide lower-course shingles under any upper-course shingles left partially nailed, and then nail them down. *Tip: Install roof jacks, if needed, after filling out the fifth course.*

Check the alignment of the shingles after each four-course cycle. In several spots on the last installed course, measure from the bottom edge of a shingle to the nearest felt paper line. If you discover any misalignment, make minor adjustments over the next few rows until it's corrected.

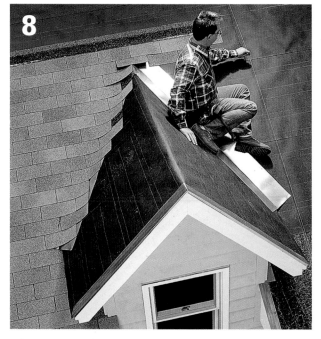

When you reach obstructions, such as dormers, install a full course of shingles above them so you can retain your shingle offset pattern. On the unshingled side of the obstruction, snap another vertical reference line using the shingles above the obstruction as a guide.

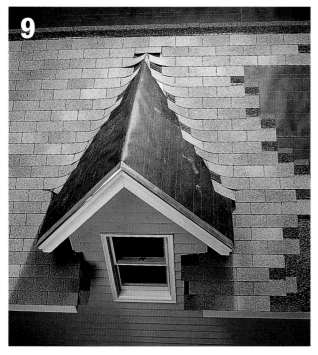

Shingle upward from the eaves on the unshingled side of the obstruction using the vertical line as a reference for re-establishing your shingle slot offset pattern. Fill out the shingle courses past the rake edges of the roof, then trim off the excess.

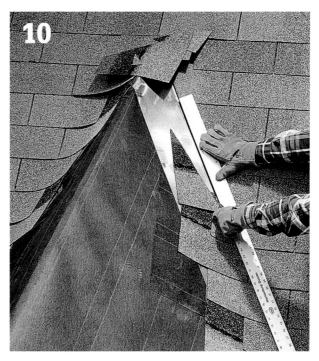

Trim off excess shingle material at the V in the valley flashing using a utility knife and straightedge. Do not cut into the flashing. The edges will be trimmed back farther at a slight taper after both roof decks are completely shingled.

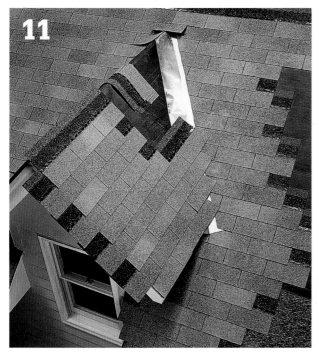

Install shingles on adjoining roof decks, starting at the bottom edge using the same offset alignment pattern shown in steps 1 to 6. Install shingles until courses overlap the center of the valley flashing. Trim shingles at both sides of the valley when finished.

Install shingles up to the vent pipe so the flashing rests on at least one row of shingles. Apply a heavy double bead of roofing cement along the bottom edge of the flange.

(continued)

13

Sleeve

14

Place the flashing over the vent pipe. Position the flashing collar so the longer portion of the tapered neck slopes down the roof and the flange lies over the shingles. Nail the perimeter of the flange using rubber gasket nails.

Cut shingles to fit around the neck of the flashing so they lie flat against the flange. Do not drive roofing nails through the flashing. Instead, apply roofing cement to the back of shingles where they lie over the flashing.

15

Base flashing

Outline of shape for first piece of step flashing

Trim line

Waste section

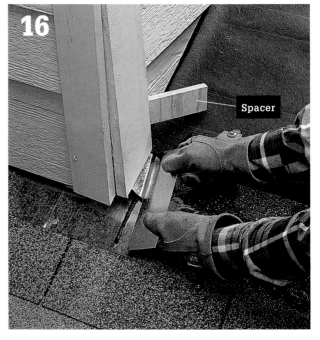

16

Spacer

Shingle up to an element that requires flashing so the top of the reveal areas are within 5" of the element. Install base flashing using the old base flashing as a template. Bend a piece of step flashing in half and set it next to the lowest corner of the element. Mark a trim line on the flashing, following the vertical edge of the element. Cut the flashing to fit.

Pry out the lowest courses of siding and any trim at the base of the element. Insert spacers to prop the trim or siding away from the work area. Apply roofing cement to the base flashing in the area where the overlap with the step flashing will be formed. Tuck the trimmed piece of step flashing under the propped area, and secure the flashing. Fasten the flashing with one rubber gasket nail driven near the top and into the roof deck.

17

Apply roofing cement to the top side of the first piece of step flashing where it will be covered by the next shingle course. Install the shingle by pressing it firmly into the roofing cement. Do not nail through the flashing underneath.

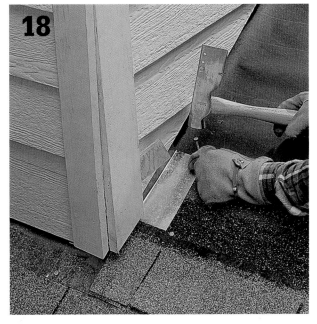

18

Tuck another piece of flashing under the trim or siding, overlapping the first piece of flashing at least 2". Set the flashing into roofing cement applied on the top of the shingle. Nail the shingle in place without driving nails through the flashing. Install flashing up to the top of the element the same way. Trim the last piece of flashing to fit the top corner of the element. Reattach the siding and trim.

19

Counterflashing

Base flashing

Shingle up to the chimney base. Use the old base flashing as a template to cut new flashing. Bend up the counter flashing. Apply roofing cement to the base of the chimney and the shingles just below the base. Press the base flashing into the roofing cement and bend the flashing around the edges of the chimney. Drive rubber gasket nails through the flashing flange into the roof deck.

20

Step flashing

Install step flashing and shingles, working up to the high side of the chimney. Fasten flashing to the chimney with roofing cement. Fold down the counter flashing as you go.

(continued)

Cut and install top flashing (also called a saddle) around the high side of the chimney. Overlap the final piece of flashing along each side. Attach the flashing with roofing cement applied to the deck and chimney and with rubber gasket nails driven through the flashing base into the roof deck. Shingle past the chimney using roofing cement (not nails) to attach shingles over the flashing.

When you reach a hip or ridge, shingle up the first side until the top of the uppermost reveal area is within 5" of the hip or ridge. Trim the shingles along the peak. Install shingles on the opposite side of the hip or ridge. Overlap the peak no more than 5".

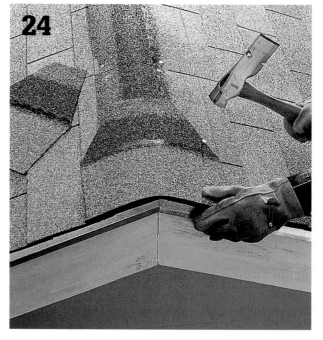

Cut three 12"-sq. cap shingles from each three-tab shingle. With the back surface facing up, cut the shingles at the tab lines. Trim the top corners of each square with an angled cut, starting just below the seal strip to avoid overlaps in the reveal area.

Snap a chalk line 6" down from the ridge, parallel to the peak. Attach cap shingles, starting at one end of the ridge, aligned with the chalk line. Drive two 1¼" roofing nails per cap about 1" from each edge, just below the seal strip.

25

Following the chalk line, install cap shingles halfway along the ridge, creating a 5" reveal for each cap. Then, starting at the opposite end, install caps over the other half of the ridge to meet the first run in the center. Cut a 5"-wide section from the reveal area of a shingle tab, and use it as a "closure cap" to cover the joint where the caps meet.

26

Shingle the hips in the same manner using a chalk reference line and cap shingles. Start at the bottom of each hip and work to the peak. Where hips join with roof ridges, install a custom shingle cut from the center of a cap shingle. Set the cap at the end of the ridge and bend the corners so they fit over the hips. Secure each corner with a roofing nail, and cover the nail heads with roofing cement.

27

After all shingles are installed, trim them at the valleys to create a gap that's 3" wide at the top and widens at a rate of ⅛" per foot as it moves downward. Use a utility knife and straightedge to cut the shingles, making sure not to cut through the valley flashing. At the valleys, seal the undersides and edges of shingles with roofing cement. Also cover exposed nail heads with roofing cement.

28

Mark and trim the shingles at the rake edges of the roof. Snap a chalk line ⅜" from the edge to make an overhang, then trim the shingles.

Installing Laminated Shingles: Pyramid Variation

Some manufacturers of laminated shingles do not recommend using the staggered installation method shown on pages 76 to 83. It requires that shingles in every other course be lifted up to slide the adjacent shingle into place. Lifting or bending laminated shingles, which are less flexible, can damage them. Instead of using this method of working off of vertical reference lines (see photo 5, page 78), you can install laminated shingles in a diagonal, pyramid-style pattern. It's an efficient alternative that doesn't require snapping vertical control lines or lifting partially installed shingles.

The diagonal pyramid effect is created by starting successive rows with incrementally smaller starter shingles. For the shingles shown here (39½" long) a set of five starter shingles was cut, each 7" shorter than the previous. Thus, starter shingle lengths were 39½", 32½", 25½", 18½", and 11½". For shingles styles where you must maintain a regular tab offset pattern, use starter shingles that increase in length by one-half tab per row.

Begin the installation process by snapping a chalk line for your starter course and nailing the starter course shingles in place. Trim and nail the starter shingles just as you would for a staggered installation along the full length of the bottom eave. Next, nail the full-length shingle of the first starter set over the starter course shingles, at the roof deck corner where two eaves meet. Position and nail the other starter set shingles above the first so the edges overhang the rake by ¾ to 1½". This will create a diagonal pattern along the exposed ends of the starter set. Now, abut and nail two full shingles beside each of the starter set shingles to extend the diagonal pattern farther. Nail a second starter set above the first along the rake edge, and add a full shingle next to each of the second starter set shingles.

Once two starter sets and their abutting shingles are in place, continue to nail the first nine courses of shingles across the roof to the other end. Work from the bottom up to lay and nail the shingles as you go. When these courses are completed, add third and fourth starter sets above the completed courses and repeat the shingling process to install the next nine courses of shingles. Work your way up the roof in this fashion until you reach the ridge, and then install ridge cap shingles as usual.

How to Install Shingles with the Pyramid Method

Cut starter strips roughly 6" wide and nail them in a row at the eave, overhang the drip edge very slightly.

Cut a set of starter shingles that decrease in size incrementally from the full length (see discussion above). For this 39½" long architectural shingle, additional start shingles were created in the following lengths: 32½", 25½", 18½", and 11½". Be sure to place a hard backerboard underneath shingles before cutting.

Nail the full-length shingle of the starter set in place, overlapping the starter course shingles at the roof deck corner. Then position and nail the remaining four starter set shingles above the first in decreasing sizes to create a diagonal pattern on the open ends.

Position and nail two full-length shingles next to each of the starter set shingles to begin the first five shingle courses. Keep the reveals even as you go along.

Add the second starter set above the first one, just as you did in step 3. Position and nail a single full shingle next to each of these starter set shingles. This initiates the next four courses of shingles.

Working from the bottom up and horizontally, position and nail additional shingles to complete the first nine courses to the opposite roof eave. Trim off the ends so they overhang the far eave by ¾ to 1½" (if you have a metal edge, shingles may remain flush, but check with the manufacturer recommendations). Repeat the process of cutting and adding starter sets, and the shingle courses they establish, until you reach the ridge. Once the opposite roof deck is shingled, install ridge cap shingles as usual (see pages 82 to 83).

Ridge Vents

If you need attic ventilation, installing a continuous ridge vent will get the job done. Since they're installed along the entire ridge of the roof, they provide an even flow of air along the entire underside of the roof decking. Combined with continuous soffit vents, this is the most effective type of ventilation system.

Since the vents are installed along the ridge, they're practically invisible, eliminating any disruptions to the roof. Other vent types, such as roof louvers and turbines, often distract from the roof's aesthetics.

Installing one continuous ridge vent is quicker and easier than installing other types of vents that need to be placed in several locations across the roof. It also saves you from having to make numerous cuts in your finished roof, which can disturb surrounding shingles.

Continuous ridge vents work in conjunction with the soffits to allow airflow under the roof decking. Installed at the roof peak and covered with cap shingles, ridge vents are less conspicuous than other roof vents.

Tools & Materials ▸

Hammer	Flat pry bar
Circular saw	Ridge vents
Tape measure	1½" roofing nails
Chalk line	

How to Install a Ridge Vent

Remove the ridge caps using a flat pry bar. Measure down from the peak the width of the manufacturer's recommended opening, and mark each end of the roof. Snap a chalk line between the marks. Repeat for the other side of the peak. Remove any nails in your path.

Set the blade depth of a circular saw to cut the sheathing but not the rafters. Cut along each chalk line, staying 12" from the edges of the roof. Remove the cut sheathing using a pry bar.

Measure down from the peak half the width of the ridge vent, and make a mark on both ends of the roof. Snap a line between the marks. Do this on both sides of the peak.

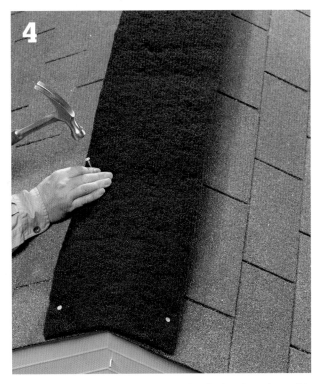

Center the ridge vent over the peak, aligning the edges with the chalk lines. Install using roofing nails that are long enough to penetrate the roof sheathing. *Tip: If a chimney extends through the peak, leave 12" of sheathing around the chimney.*

Butt sections of ridge vents together and nail the ends. Install vents across the entire peak, including the 12" sections at each end of the roof that were not cut away.

Place ridge cap shingles over the ridge vents. Nail them with two 1½" roofing nails per cap. Overlap the caps as you would on a normal ridge. If the caps you removed in step 1 are still in good shape, you can reuse them. Otherwise, use new ones.

Shingling Over an Old Roof

Installing shingles over your current shingles saves you the time, labor, and expense of tearing off the old roof covering. This method certainly has its appeal, but there's still some preparation work involved. Make any necessary repairs to the roof decking before applying new shingles. Replace any missing shingles, and renail any loose ones. Drive down protruding nails so the heads won't pierce the new roofing materials.

In order to shingle over old roofing, you cannot have more than one or two layers of shingles already on the roof, depending on your building codes. If you already have the maximum number of layers, the old shingles will need to be completely removed. To check for underlying shingles, lift up the shingles along the rake or eaves end of the roof and count the number of layers.

Before starting the project, read the section on shingling a roof, pages 76 to 83.

Before starting the project, read the section on shingling a roof, pages 76 to 83.

Tools & Materials ▶

Aviation snips
Carpenter's square
Chalk line
Flat pry bar
Roofer's hatchet or pneumatic nailer
Utility knife
Straightedge
Tape measure
Flashing
Shingles
Roofing cement
Roofing nails

Installing shingles over an old roof is frowned upon in some quarters, primarily because it does not allow you to inspect the roof deck and underlayment. But if your old roof is in good condition, most municipalities will allow you to add one new layer (but not more than that) of shingles over the old roof.

How to Shingle Over an Old Roof

Cut tabs off shingles and install the remaining strips over the reveal area of the old first course, creating a flat surface for the starter row of new shingles. Use roofing nails that are long enough to penetrate the roof decking by at least ¾".

Trim the top of shingles for the first course. The shingles should be sized to butt against the bottom edge of the old third course, overhanging the roof edge by ½". Install shingles so the tab slots don't align with the slots in the old shingles.

Using the old shingles to direct your layout, begin installing the new shingles. Maintain a consistent tab/slot offset if you are installing three-tab shingles. Shingle up toward the roof ridge, stopping before the final course. Install flashing as you proceed.

Flashing is installed using the same techniques and materials as shingling over felt paper, except that you need to trim or fill in shingles around vent pipes and roof vents to create a flat surface for the base flange of the flashing pieces. *Tip: Valley flashing in good condition does not have to be replaced. Replace any other old flashing as you go.*

Tear off old hip and ridge caps before shingling these areas. Replace with new ridge caps after all other shingling has been completed.

Cedar Shakes

Cedar shakes (which are thick and rough) and shingles (which are tapered and smooth) are installed in much the same way, with one major difference. Shakes have felt paper installed between each course, while shingles do not. Shingles are often applied over open sheathing, while shakes are installed over open or solid sheathing. Air circulation under shakes and shingles can increase their life span. Check your local building codes to see what type of sheathing is recommended for your area.

The gaps between shakes and shingles, called joints, are specified by the manufacturer. You can determine how much of the material to leave exposed below the overlap, as long as it falls within the manufacturer's guidelines.

Tools & Materials ▸

Roofer's hatchet	30# felt paper
Tape measure	Stapler
Utility knife	Mason's string
Stapler	Roofing cement
Chalk line	
Circular saw	
Jigsaw	
Caulk gun	
Shakes	
Flashing	
Nails	

A shake roof's irregular pattern and earth tone colors produce a more pleasing, organic effect than the brick-laid uniformity of asphalt shingles. These days, shakes can be made of cedar, steel, or various synthetic materials. Installation methods will vary with each material type.

Cedar Shakes & Shingles

Wood shakes and shingles are available in different grades. Some of the more popular include resawn shake (A), No. 1 hand-split medium shake (B), standard-grade shake (C), taper-sawn shake (D), No. 1 heavy shake (E), pressure-treated medium shake (F), No. 2 shingle (G), undercoursing shingle (H), No. 1 shingle (I).

Underlayment for Cedar Shakes & Shingles

Spaced sheathing is common, and sometimes required, for cedar shakes and shingles. Solid sheathing is installed along the eaves and rake ends, and open-spaced wood strips are installed in the field to allow for air circulation.

To install spacer strips over solid sheathing, place 2 × 4s flat over each rafter and nail them to the roof. Nail 1 × 4 or 1 × 6 nailing strips across the 2 × 4s. Keep the strips together along the eaves, then space them at a distance equal to the exposure rate in the field.

How to Install Cedar Shakes

Prepare the roof decking by installing valley flashing at all valleys (page 75). Apply felt paper underlayment to the first 36" of the roof deck. *Note: Depending on your climate and building codes, you may want to install ice and water shield for this step rather than felt paper.*

Install a starter shake so it overhangs the eaves and rake edge by 1½". Do the same on the opposite side of the roof. Run a taut string between the bottom edges of the two shakes. Install the remaining shakes in the starter row, aligning the bottoms with the string. Keep the manufacturer's recommended distance between shakes, usually ⅜ to ⅝".

Set the first course of shakes over the starter row, aligning the shakes along the rake ends and bottoms. Joints between shakes must overlap by at least 1½". Drive two nails in each shake, ¾ to 1" from the edges, and 1½ to 2" above the exposure line. Use the hatchet to rip shakes to fit. *Tip: Set the gauge on your roofer's hatchet to the exposure rate. You can then use the hatchet as a quick reference for checking the exposure.*

Snap a chalk line over the first course of shakes at the exposure line. Snap a second line at a distance that's twice the exposure rate. Staple an 18"-wide strip of felt paper at the second line. Overlap felt paper vertical seams by 4". Install the second course of shakes at the exposure line, offsetting joints by 1½" minimum. Install remaining courses the same way.

Set shakes in place along valleys, but don't nail them. Hold a 1 × 4 against the center of the valley flashing without nailing it. Place it over the shakes to use as a guide for marking the angle of the valley. Cut the shakes using a circular saw, then install.

Use the 1 × 4 to align the edge of the shakes along the valley. Keep the 1 × 4 butted against the valley center, and place the edge of the shake along the edge of the board. Avoid nailing through the valley flashing when installing the shakes.

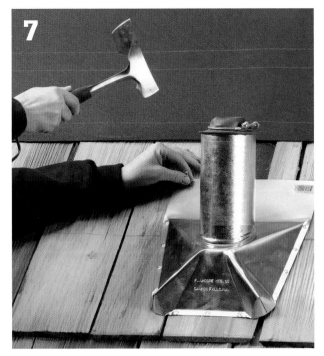

Notch shakes to fit around a plumbing stack using a jigsaw, then install a course of shakes below the stack. Apply roofing cement to the underside of the stack flashing, then place it over the stack and over the shakes. Nail the flashing along the edges.

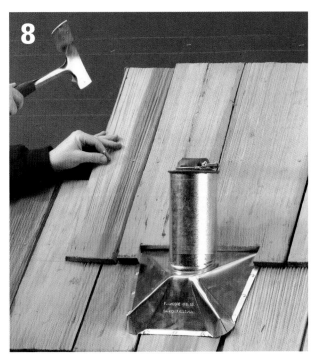

Overlap the exposed flashing with the next row of shakes. Cut notches in the shakes to fit around the stack, keeping a 1" gap between the stack and shakes.

(continued)

9

Install shakes under the bottom apron flashing beneath a skylight. Cut the shakes as necessary. Nail the shakes without driving nails through the flashing. Apply roofing cement to the underside of the flashing, then press to the shakes.

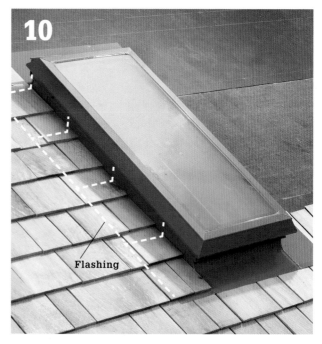

10

Flashing

Interweave skylight flashing along the skylight with rows of shakes. After each row of shakes, install a piece of flashing with the vertical plane placed under the edge lip of the skylight and the horizontal plane flush with the bottom edge of the shake. A row of shakes covers the top apron flashing.

11

Apply roofing cement along the underside of the roof louver flange, then set it over the vent cutout and over the shakes directly below it. Nail the louver in place. Install shakes over the sides and back of the louver, trimming to fit as needed.

12

As you approach the ridge, measure from the last installed row to the peak. Do this on each side of the roof. If the measurements are not equal, slightly adjust the exposure rate in successive rows until the measurements are the same. Make sure you're measuring to points that are aligned at the peak. The top of the sheathing is probably not level across the roof and cannot be a reference point.

Run shakes past the roof peak. Snap a chalk line across the shakes at the ridge. Set the circular saw blade to the depth of the shakes, then cut along the chalk line.

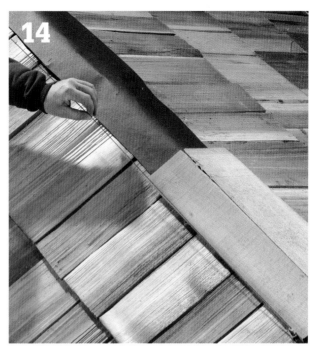

Cut 8" strips of felt paper and staple them over the hips and ridge. Set a factory-made hip and ridge cap at one end of the ridge, aligned with the roof peak. Do the same at the other end of the roof. Snap a chalk line between the outside edges of the caps.

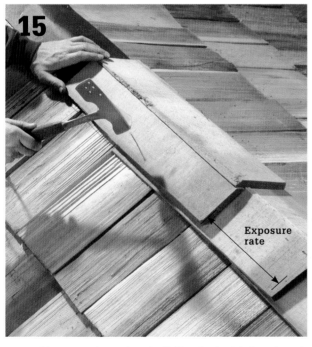

Exposure rate

Set a ridge cap along the chalk line flush with the edge of the roof to serve as the starter. Install with two nails. Place a cap directly on top of the starter cap, and nail in place. Install caps along the remainder of the ridge, alternating the overlap pattern. The exposure rate should be the same as the roof shakes. Nails should penetrate the roof decking by ½".

Variation: If the ridge caps are not preassembled by the manufacturer, install the first cap along the chalk line, then place the second cap over the edge of the first. Alternate the overlap pattern across the ridge.

Roll Roofing

Roll roofing is a quick and easy roofing product to install. The material is simply rolled across the roof, nailed along the edges, and sealed with roofing cement. It's geared for roofs with slight slopes, such as porches and garages.

Some manufacturers recommend using a roof primer prior to installing the roofing. Read and follow manufacturer's directions. Your roof decking must be completely clean before the roll roofing can be applied. Any debris, even a small twig or leaf, can end up showing through the roofing.

Store the roofing in a warm, dry location until you're ready to start the project, and choose a warm day for the installation. Roll roofing is best installed in temperatures above 45°F. If applied in cold weather, the material can crack.

The following pages show the three methods for installing roll roofing. The perimeter bond application, pages 97 to 98, is the fastest installation method and can be used on sloped roofs. The concealed nail application, page 99, is best for roofs with a slighter pitch all the way down to a 1-in-12 slope, because it prevents water from penetrating under the nail heads. The double coverage method, also on page 99, is used for roofs that are almost completely flat. The double coverage, using fully bonded selvedge roofing, offers better protection against water infiltration.

Tools & Materials ▸

Utility knife
Tape measure
Chalk line
Serrated trowel
Straightedge
Hammer

Roll roofing
Galvanized
   roofing nails
Asphalt-based
   roofing cement

Roll roofing is used on roofs that have a slight slope. Installation is fast and straightforward, with the material rolled over a clean roof decking.

How to Install Roll Roofing (Perimeter Bond)

Nail drip edge along the eaves and rake ends of the roof (pages 72 to 73). Sweep the roof decking clean. Center an 18"-wide strip of roll roofing over the valley. Nail one side ¾" from the edge, every 6". Press the roofing firmly into the valley center, then nail the other side. Install a 36" strip over the valley the same way.

Snap a chalk line 35½" up from the eaves. Unroll the roofing along the chalk line, overhanging the eaves and rake edges by ½". Nail the roofing every 3" along the sides and bottom, ¾" from the edge of the decking. Roofing nails should be long enough to penetrate the roof decking by at least ¾".

Where more than one roll is needed to complete a course, apply roofing cement along the edge of the installed piece using a trowel. Place a new roll 6" over the first piece. Press the seam together and drive nails every 3" along the end lap. *Tip: Make sure the roofing is straight before nailing. Once it's nailed, you can't adjust it without creating wrinkles and folds. If it's running crooked, cut it and start with a new strip.*

Apply 2" of roofing cement along the top edge of the installed course. Install the second row flush with the line on the roofing, overlapping the cement edge. Drive nails every 3" along the rakes and overlap, ¾" from the edges. Do the same for remaining rows, offsetting seams at least 18".

(continued)

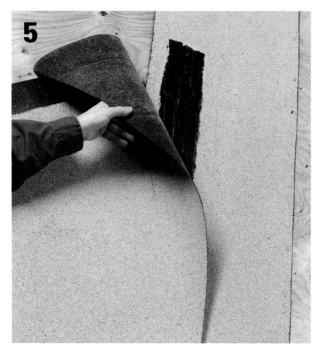

Cut roofing 1" from the valley center using a utility knife and straightedge. Be careful not to cut into the valley roofing. Apply a 6"-wide strip of roofing cement on the valley at the overlap. Place the main roofing over the cement. Nail in place every 3" along the seam.

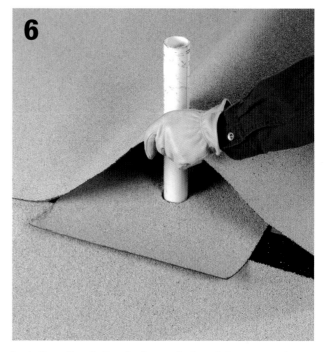

Install roofing in front of a vent pipe. Cut a square of roofing to fit over the pipe, with a hole in the center. Apply roofing cement around the edges of the square, then set it in place over the pipe. Overlap with the next row of roofing, notching for the pipe as necessary.

Cut the roofing flush with the roof peak. Snap a line on each side of the roof, 5½" from the peak. Apply 2" of cement above each line. Place a 12"-wide strip of roofing over the peak, flush with the chalk lines. Drive nails every 3" along the seams, ¾" from the edges. *Tip: Use modest amounts of roofing cement. Excess cement can cause the roofing to blister.*

Variation: Rather than install a strip over the ridge, extend the roofing on one side of the roof 6" past the peak, overlapping the opposite side. Nail along the edge to secure it to the decking. Do the same on the other side, overlapping the installed roofing at the peak. Apply cement along the seam, and nail in place.

How to Install Roll Roofing (Concealed Nail Application)

Cut 9"-wide strips of roofing. Nail them in place along the rakes and eaves. Snap a chalk line 35½" up from the eaves. Place the first course of roofing flush with the line.

Nail the roofing along the top edge only, driving nails every 4", ¾" from the top edge. Roll back the side and bottom edges. Apply cement along the outside 2" of the strips installed in step 1. Set the overlapping strip back in place, pressing firmly to seal.

Set the next course in place so it overlaps the first row by 4". Nail along the top edge. Lift the side and bottom edges, apply cement, then press together to seal. Repeat this process for the remainder of the roof.

How to Install Roll Roofing (Double Coverage Application)

Cut away the granular part of the roofing to create a starter strip. Align the strip with the eaves, and drive nails along the top and bottom edge at 12" intervals. Place the first full course flush with the eaves. Nail the nongranule edges every 12". Roll back the bottom of the roofing and apply roofing cement along the eaves and rake edges on the starter strips. Set the roofing back in place, pressing it into the cement.

Align the bottom edge of the second course with the top of the granule edge of the first row. Nail every 12" along the nongranule edges. Flip the bottom part back, apply cement along the sides and bottom of the nongranule area of the first course, then set the strip back in place. Install remaining courses the same way.

EPDM Rubber Roofing

For roof decks with minimal pitch, even rolled asphalt roofing may not offer enough protection against leaks. In these situations, ethylene propylene diene monomer (EPDM) rubber membrane roofing may be your best—or only—bet. EPDM roofing is easy to install with minimal tools by a do-it-yourselfer. Unlike other membrane systems that must be applied with a torch, EPDM adheres with liquid adhesive. It comes in 10 × 20- or 20 × 100-feet rolls so you can plan your installation to minimize seams.

Installing the membrane involves removing the previous roofing material down to bare roof decking and any flashings around vent pipes or other protrusions. Make sure your roof deck material is clean, dry, and in good repair. You may be able to overlay the deck with a layer of high-density fiberboard or 1-inch isocyanurate insulation board to create a fresh, flat deck surface if the previous surface isn't sufficiently flat or shows signs of minor deterioration. Avoid using insulation products with a waterproofing layer or film. Glue will not penetrate properly into the insulation.

Once the deck is prepared, lay out the membrane sheets so they overlap the edges of the roof and one another by 3 inches. Make any necessary cutouts to allow for roof protrusions and to allow the membrane sheets to lay flat and relax. If your roof abuts a vertical wall, the membrane should extend up the wall 12 inches so it can be adhered to the wall and sealed with a metal termination bar.

Adhering the membrane to the roof deck involves applying liquid bonding adhesive onto the roof deck with the membrane rolled back, allowing it to partially cure, then pressing the membrane into place over the adhesive, and brushing it thoroughly to remove any air pockets. Once the membrane is fixed in place, you seal the overlapping seams with strips of soft seaming tape and liquid primer, rolling the seams flat. Finish up the roof by trimming the membrane at the roof edges, installing the appropriate boot flashings, and adding any termination bars that may be required.

Follow the EPDM manufacturer's instructions carefully, particularly if they differ from the step-by-step process you see here.

Tools & Materials ▸

Measuring tape	Liquid adhesive
Paint roller	Seaming tape
Stiff-bristle push broom	Primer
Utility knife	Contact cement
J-roller or roller seaming tool	Termination bars (if applicable)
EPDM membrane	Exterior screws

EPDM roofing provides the best protection against leaks on low-pitched roofs. It's an easy-to-install, DIY project. Most home centers now carry rubber roofing in standard 10 x 20 ft. sheets for less than $100. Some also will sell 10-ft. wide roofing by the linear foot from a longer roll. When possible, buy a large enough sheet to cover the entire roof. This greatly decreases the likelihood of leaks forming because it eliminates the need to seam the roof covering.

Rubber roof coverings require special adhesives and primers, as well as flashing and accessories such as rubber pipe boots. Shown here, from left to right, are pipe boots (A), EPDM adhesive and primer (B, C), hose clamp (D), insulation plates (E), termination bars (F), exterior screws (G), caulk (H), seaming tape (I), EPDM membrane (J), and J-roller (K).

Most rubber roofs are fully bonded to a substrate of insulation board, but they can also be bonded directly to a plywood roof deck or even installed with a perimeter bond only. In some commercial applications they are installed with a layer of river rock on top for ballast.

How to Install an EPDM Rubber Roof

Prepare the roof deck for membrane roofing by removing the old roofing material down to bare decking. Look closely for signs of deterioration. Replace deteriorated decking. For a smooth surface, cover the roof with a new layer of high-density fiberboard (sold at roofing materials suppliers). Secure with fasteners recommended by the manufacturer for this purpose—usually long screws with large insulation plates.

Sweep the roof deck thoroughly, and spread out the membrane so it has a chance to relax. Make any cutouts in the membrane that may be necessary to allow for vent pipes or other protrusions. Overlap the sheets by 3" and wipe them down with the recommended cleaner to prepare the surfaces for adhesive.

Apply the latex adhesive. Fold half of the first membrane sheet over on itself to expose the roof deck, and roll a heavy coat of adhesive onto both the deck and membrane surfaces with a medium-nap paint roller. However, do not apply adhesive to the overlapped section of membrane. Once the adhesive begins to set (about 20 minutes in normal conditions), carefully roll the folded rubber down into place. Avoid wrinkling the membrane.

Use a stiff-bristle push broom to brush out any air pockets that may be evident under the bonded half of the membrane. Brush from the middle of the roof outward to the edges. Then fold the other unbonded half over, apply adhesive to the rubber and roof deck again, and adhere this half of the membrane to the roof. Apply all sections of membrane to the roof deck in this fashion, but do not apply adhesive within 3" of the edges of any overlapping sections of rubber; these must be accessible for applying seaming tape along the seams.

Roll the top section of overlapping membrane back along the seam area, and chalk a reference line 3" from the edge of the bottom membrane. This marks the area for applying seaming tape.

Tape the seams. Use the recommended cleaning solvent to clean both halves of the overlapping membrane in the tape areas, then apply seaming tape sticky side down to the bottom membrane within the marked area. Press the tape down firmly to ensure good adhesion to the membrane.

Fold the top membrane overlap back in place on the tape. Slowly pull off the tape's paper backing with the membrane edges now overlapping. Press the overlapping edges down to create a tighter, smooth seam. Roll the seamed areas with a J-roller or seam rolling tool to bond the seam.

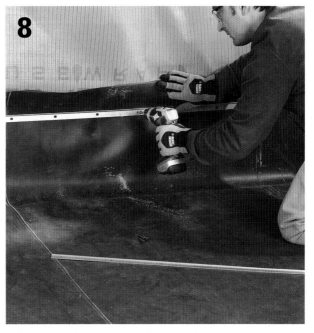

If the roof meets a vertical wall, you may need to remove siding so you can bond the membrane to wall sheathing. Use contact adhesive to apply the membrane 12" up the wall. Seal the edge with a metal termination bar fastened to the wall with exterior screws. Trim off overhanging membrane around the roof edges, and flash it according to the manufacturer's recommendations using rubber adhesive flashing and rubber boots.

Tile Roofing

Modern clay tiles use an S-type design rather than the two-piece system that was once common. This simplifies the installation process and saves you time. Due to the contour of the tiles, you'll need plumbing vents and air vents that match the shape of the roofing materials.

Before starting the project, make sure your roof framing can support the weight of the tiles. The materials are very heavy, and roofs designed for asphalt shingles may not have the structural support for clay tile. Check with your building inspector if you're unsure.

Tools & Materials ▸

Hammer	Sand
Tape measure	Portland cement
Chalk line	Plastic cement
Circular saw	Cement mortar
Jigsaw	Type M
Trowel	Tile
Diamond saw blade	Bird stops
Caulk gun	Plumbing vents
30# felt paper	Air vents
Ice and water shield	Roofing sealant
Nailers (2 × 6, 2 × 3,	Peel-and-stick
2 × 2)	flashing
¾" roofing nails	Plastic cement
Roofing nails	

Tips for Installing a Tile Roof ▸

To cut clay tile, use a diamond blade in a circular saw or grinder. Clamp the tile to a work surface, make your cutting line on the tile, then cut along the line. Be sure to wear safety glasses and a respirator when making the cuts.

Mortar is available premixed, or you can mix it yourself. This project requires cement mortar Type M. To mix it, combine 3 parts portland cement, 1 part lime, and 12 parts sand. Add water and mix until the consistency is like mashed potatoes.

Clay tiles give homes a truly impressive roof that can't be imitated by other materials. The S design makes installation easier and less time-consuming. Each tile simply overlaps the preceding tile (below).

How to Install a Tile Roof

Cover the roof with underlayment (pages 70 to 71). Install drip edge (pages 72 to 73) and valley flashing (page 75). Nail 2 × 6 lumber on the edge over all ridges and hips.

Install 2 × 2 nailers along the rake edges of the roof. Butt 2 × 3 nailers against the 2 × 2s and nail them in place.

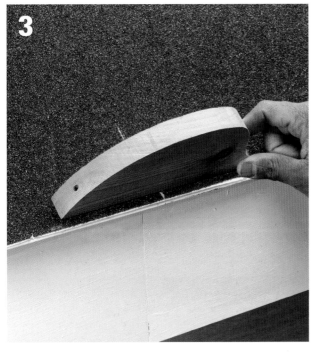

Measuring from the outside edge of the 2 × 3 nailer along the left rake edge, make marks on the roof every 12". Center a bird stop over each mark, aligned with the front edge of the roof, and nail in place. *Note: Bird stops are available from the tile manufacturer, or you can cut your own from wood.*

Place gable tile over the 2 × 2s along the rake ends of the roof, overhanging the front of the roof by 3". Nail in place, using two ¾" roofing nails per tile. Overlap tiles by 3". *Note: Be sure to use left gable tiles for the left side and right gable tiles for the right side.*

(continued)

Starting on the left side of the roof, place the first field tile over the gable tile and 2 × 3 nailer. Align the end of the field tile with the end of the gable tile. Nail in place with two nails. Install the first course of tiles the same way, placing them over the bird stops. *Tip: To ensure alignment, tie a string across the end of the first gable tiles. Set the tiles flush with the string. Move the string to align subsequent rows.*

Install the next row of tiles on the roof, overlapping the first course by 3". Install remaining courses the same way. Avoid stepping on or walking on tiles as they break easily. When you can no longer reach new tiles from below, begin to work from higher up the roof. Work around obstacles as you encounter them, as seen in the remaining photos.

At dormers, chimneys, and walls, install pan flashing at least 4" up the wall and a minimum of 6" along the roof. Turn up the outside edge of the flashing 1½". Install counter flashing over the pan flashing. *Note: The top edge of the counter flashing must be installed under the wall siding or placed in the mortar between bricks in the chimney. The flashing may still be present from the old roof.*

Install a 2 × 3 nailer along the turned-up edge of the pan flashing. Set the tile over the nailer and nail it in place.

9

When the roofing abuts a wall of the house, install tile up the roof to the wall. Apply mortar generously between the tops of the tiles and the wall, filling in any gaps. Place 3 × 4 flashing over the mortar, then place counter flashing over that.

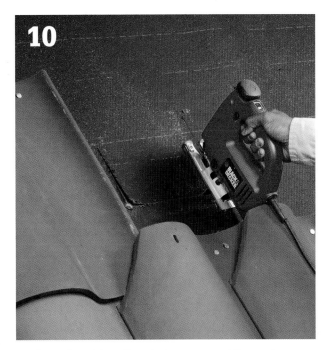

10

Mark roof vent locations between rows of tiles and between rafters. Follow manufacturer's guidelines for the size of the opening. Cut out the opening using a jigsaw or circular saw. *Tip: Periodically look at the roof from the street to make sure the rows are running straight and the tiles look uniform.*

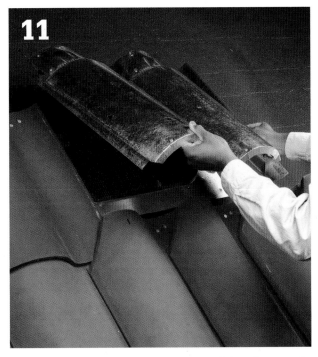

11

Apply roofing sealant along the bottom of the primary roof vent, then install it over the opening using roofing nails driven every 4" through the flange. Seal the flange with peel-and-stick flashing. Place the secondary vent over the primary vent and nail it to the roof. Overlap the lip with the next piece of tile.

12

Center ridge tiles over the hips and peak. Apply a small amount of plastic cement on the nose of each ridge tile. Overlap the tiles for a 16" exposure, placing the tile over the plastic cement on the previous tile. Nail the ridge tiles using two nails per tile. Fill the gaps beneath ridge tiles with mortar (inset photo).

Installing Siding

Few other exterior improvements will give your home such a dramatic facelift as new siding. Siding allows you to change both the color and texture of outside walls. If you're tired of your current faded aluminum siding or you can't bear the thought of spending next July scraping and painting wood clapboard again, maybe it's time to switch to low-maintenance vinyl or fiber-cement lap siding. Siding products have come a long way in the past few decades, and your choices of colors and styles have never been greater. For a warmer, more rustic look, consider siding your home with cypress shakes or a cedar board and batten treatment, and then accent your foundation with veneered stone or brick. Wrapping a home with vinyl or wood is well within a seasoned do-it-yourselfer's capabilities. And when you're through, both you and the neighbors can appreciate your handiwork for many decades to come.

If you have a basic collection of hand and power tools, you've got most of the hardware needed for the job already. Be sure to read other sections in this book that cover working safely at heights. Do a careful job of sheathing and wrapping your home to keep moisture outside where it belongs. Then get ready for a big project that will pay dividends in the end.

In this chapter:

- Siding Tools & Materials
- Removing Siding
- Replacing Wall Sheathing
- Housewrap
- Vinyl Siding
- Lap Siding
- Wood Shakes & Shingles
- Board & Batten Siding
- Log Cabin Siding

Siding Tools & Materials

Basic construction and remodeling tools are all you need for wood, fiber-cement, and vinyl siding projects. If you don't have some of these cutting, measuring, or leveling tools, it's worthwhile to buy them. They're not very expensive, and you'll get a lot of use out of them for other common home improvement and repair projects.

Tools for wood and fiber-cement siding include circular saw (A), miter saw (B), T-bevel (C), jigsaw (D), level (E), coping saw (F), handsaw (G), utility knife (H), hammer (I), caulk gun (J), chalk line (K), folding tape measure (L), tape measure (M), and line level (N).

Tools for vinyl siding include circular saw (A), nail slot punch (B), caulk gun (C), framing square (D), zip tool (E), utility knife (F), hammer (G), aviation snips (H), tape measure (I), level (J), and chalk line (K).

Caulks for siding include (from left) concrete and masonry silicone caulk, concrete sealant, acrylic latex caulk, acrylic latex caulk with silicone, and elastomeric latex sealant.

Tools and materials for siding include housewrap (A), felt paper (B), cap nails (C), hammer (D), hammer stapler (E), and staple gun and staples (F).

Removing Siding

Although it's sometimes possible to install new siding over old if the old siding is solid and firmly attached to the house, in most cases it's better to remove the siding, especially if it's damaged. Taking off the old siding allows you to start with a flat, smooth surface. And because the overall thickness of the siding will remain unchanged, you won't have to add extensions to your window and door jambs.

There's no "right" way to remove siding. Each type of siding material is installed differently, and consequently, they have different removal techniques. A couple of universal rules do apply, however. Start by removing trim that's placed over the siding, and work from the top down. Siding is usually installed from the bottom up, and working in the opposite direction makes removal much easier. Determine the best removal method for your project based on your type of siding.

Strip one side of the house at a time, then re-side that wall before ripping the siding off another section. This minimizes the amount of time your bare walls are exposed to the elements. Take care not to damage the sheathing. If you can't avoid tearing the housewrap, it can easily be replaced, but the sheathing is another story.

While the goal is to remove the siding as quickly as possible, it's also important to work safely. Take care when working around windows so the siding doesn't damage the glass. Invest the necessary time to protect the flowers and shrubs before starting the tear off (page 59).

Renting a dumpster will expedite the cleanup process. It's much easier to dispose of the siding as soon as it's removed rather than stacking it up in an unsightly pile in your yard, then throwing it away later. When you're finished with your cleanup, use a release magnet to collect the nails on the ground.

Tools & Materials ▸

Cat's paw	Masonry-cutting
Flat pry bar	blade
Zip tool	Masonry bit
Drill	Aviation snips
Circular saw	Roofing shovel
Masonry chisel	Release magnet
Hammer	

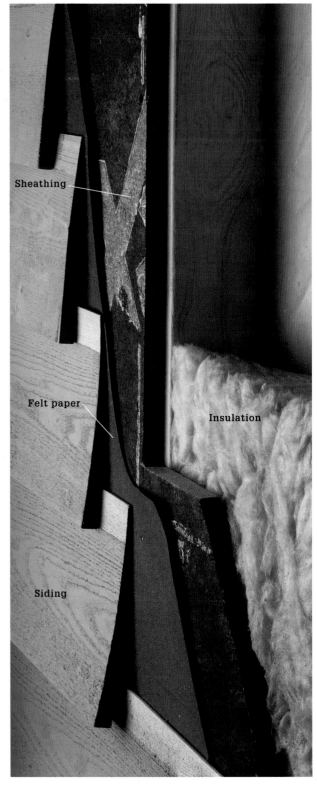

The exterior wall is composed of siding, housewrap or felt paper, and sheathing. Try to remove the siding without disturbing or damaging the sheathing.

Tips for Removing Siding

Brick molding comes preattached to most wood-frame window and door units. To remove the molding, pry along the outside of the frame to avoid marring the exposed parts of the jambs and molding.

Lap siding is nailed at the top, then covered by the next course. Pry off the trim at the top of the wall to expose the nails in the top row. Remove the nails using a cat's paw, and work your way down the wall.

Shakes and shingles are best removed with a roofing shovel. Use the shovel to pry the siding away from the wall. Once the siding is removed, use the shovel or a hammer to pull out the remaining nails.

Board and batten siding is removed by prying off the battens from over the boards. Use a pry bar or cat's paw to remove the nails from the boards.

Siding shown cutaway for clarity

Vinyl siding has a locking channel that fits over the nailing strip of the underlying piece. To remove, use a zip tool to separate the panels, and use a flat pry bar or hammer to remove the nails.

Stucco

Building paper

Sheathing

Metal lath

Stucco siding is difficult to remove. It's usually much easier to apply the new siding over the stucco than to remove it. If you're determined to take it off, use a cold chisel and hammer to break it into pieces, and use aviation snips to cut the lath.

Replacing Wall Sheathing

After removing the old siding, inspect the sheathing to make sure it's still in good condition. If water has penetrated behind the siding, there's a good chance the sheathing is warped, rotted, or otherwise damaged and will need to be replaced. You'll only need to replace the section of sheathing that's damaged. Before cutting into the wall, make sure there are no wires, cables, or pipes under the sheathing.

Older homes typically have planks or plywood sheathing, while new homes may have a nonstructural sheathing. The replacement material doesn't have to be the same material as the original sheathing, but it does have to be the same thickness.

Tools & Materials ▸

Hammer
Circular saw
Tape measure
Chalk line
Pry bar
Sheathing
2 × 4
Deck screws
    (3", 2¼")
Drill

How to Replace Damaged Wall Sheathing

Mark the location of walls studs around the damaged area. With a chalk line, mark straight cutting lines around the damage, locating the lines so they fall over framing members (at least vertically). This will allow for more secure attachment of the patch area.

Cut out the damaged sheathing, following your cutting lines with a circular saw and utility blade. Set the saw cutting depth about 1/16" deeper than the sheathing thickness and extend the cuts slightly beyond the corners to ensure a square cutout.

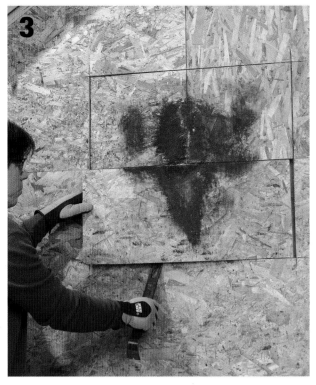

Remove the damaged sheathing materials. You may need to finish the circular saw cuts with a jigsaw or handsaw. Pry the pieces off with a pry bar if necessary.

Measure the opening, making sure the vertical cuts fall over framing members. From exterior-rated sheathing, cut a patch that's ⅛" smaller than the opening in all directions.

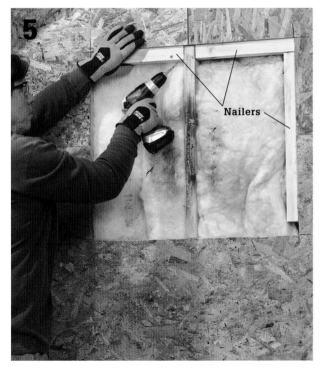

Nailers

Install 2 x 4 nailers at the top and bottom of the opening to create nailing surfaces for the patch. If the sides of the opening do no have adequate nailing surface, attach a nailer there as well.

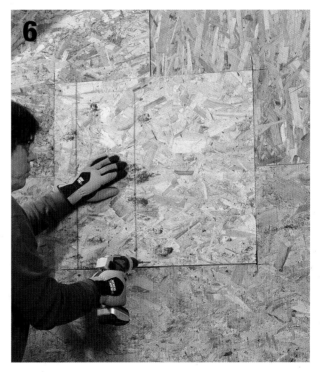

Place the new piece of sheathing in the opening, keeping a ⅛" gap on each side to allow for expansion. Attach the sheathing to the nailing strips and studs using 2¼" deck screws driven every 6 to 12".

Housewrap

Housewrap is a specially engineered fabric that blocks air and water infiltration from the outside but allows moisture vapor to pass through from the inside. It's best to apply the housewrap before installing windows and doors, but since that's not always possible with a remodeling or siding replacement job, you can cut the housewrap to fit around them. Most siding materials need to be nailed to studs, and the marks on the housewrap identify their locations. Staples are permissible for fastening housewrap, but cap nails are recommended and have better holding power.

Felt paper is not the same as housewrap. It's not necessarily designed to work as an air barrier, and it may absorb water. Do not substitute felt paper when housewrap is supposed to be used.

Tools & Materials ▸

Hammer	Cap nails
Utility knife	(2" or 3")
Tape dispenser	housewrap tape
Housewrap	

Make sure the stud marks on the housewrap are aligned with the wall studs.

How to Install Housewrap

Starting 6 to 12" around a corner and 3" over the foundation to cover the sill plate, unroll the housewrap along the side of the house with the printed side facing out. Align the printed stud marks on the housewrap with the stud marks on the sheathing. Keep the roll straight as you unwrap it.

Nail the housewrap every 12 to 18" on the vertical stud lines using cap nails. Keep the housewrap pulled snug as it's unrolled. Cut holes in the housewrap for extrusions such as hose spigots and the electric meter.

Housewrap helps protect the house from its worst enemies—water, moisture, and cold air drafts. Covering exterior walls with housewrap before installing siding can also reduce your energy bills.

3

When starting a new roll, overlap vertical seams by 6 to 12", aligning the stud marks. Begin the second course by overlapping the bottom course by 6". Once again, make sure stud marks are lined up.

4

At window and door locations, cut the housewrap at the middle of the nailing flanges. At the bottom, cut the housewrap at the sill. Pull the sill and jamb flashing over the housewrap. Be careful not to slice the nailing flanges and windowsills when cutting the housewrap.

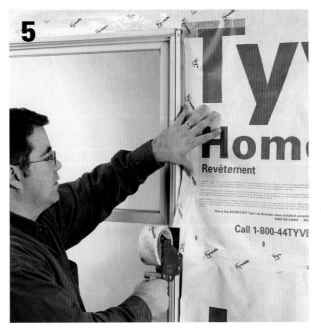

5

Tape all horizontal and vertical seams, accidental tears, and seams around doors, windows, and plumbing and electrical protrusions using housewrap tape. Tape the bottom of the protrusion first, then the sides, then place a piece of tape over the top.

Vinyl Siding

Vinyl has become one of the most popular sidings due to its low cost, uniform appearance, and maintenance-free durability. Installation is fairly simple, with each row locking onto the lip of the underlying course, then nailed along the top.

There are a couple of key factors that will make or break your siding project. First, the sheathing must be straight and solid before the siding is applied. The siding will only look as straight and smooth as the wall it's on. Second, determine how the siding should overlap to hide the seams from the main traffic patterns. This usually means starting in the back and working toward the front of the house.

Do not nail the siding tight to the house. The panels need to slide back and forth as they expand and contract with changes in the temperature. If the siding can't move, it will bow and need to be reinstalled. Keep a 1/32" gap between the head of the nail and the siding.

Vinyl siding is available in a wide variety of colors and styles, and with a lot of accessories such as trim, fluted lineals, vertical columns, crown molding, and band boards. The most common vinyl siding is horizontal lap siding, which is shown starting on page 120. This project shows a foam underlayment, which reduces outside noise, protects the siding from dents, and adds an insulation value. Vertical vinyl siding is also available. It's specifically made for vertical applications. Vinyl shakes are another type of vinyl siding, and that installation is shown on pages 126 to 127.

Tools & Materials ▸

Hammer	Zip-lock tool
Circular saw	Snap lock punch
or radial-arm saw	Caulk gun
Clamps	Vinyl siding
Tape measure	J-channel
String	Corner posts
Straightedge	Undersill
Utility knife	Starter strip
Aviation snips	Nails
Level	Cutting table
Chalk line	Safety glasses
Framing square	Silicone caulk
Nail slot punch	

Vinyl siding can look very similar to wood lap siding, but it doesn't require regular upkeep. Vinyl can be installed on any type and style of house.

Tips for Cutting Vinyl Siding

Use a fine-tooth blade installed backward in the saw to cut vinyl siding. Use a radial-arm saw, power miter saw, or a circular saw, and move the blade slowly through the siding. Always wear safety glasses when cutting siding.

Support the siding on a cutting table when cutting. Vinyl siding is too flimsy to be placed across sawhorses without support. You can build a cutting table by fastening a long piece of scrap plywood between two sawhorses.

Tips for Using Specialty Tools

A snap lock punch is used to make raised tabs, or dimples, in a cut edge of siding where the nailing hem has been removed. This eliminates the need to facenail the panel.

A nail slot punch is used to make horizontal nail slots in the face of panels. It can also be used to add or elongate the opening of an existing nail slot to match irregular stud spacing.

How to Install Vinyl Siding

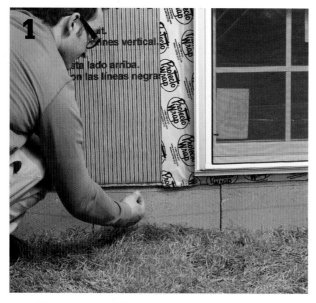

Install housewrap following instructions on pages 116 to 117. Identify the lowest corner of the house that has sheathing, and partially drive a nail 1½" above the bottom edge of the sheathing. Run a level string to the opposite corner of the wall and partially drive a nail. Do this around the entire house. Snap chalk lines between the nails.

Place the top edge of the starter strip along the chalk line and nail every 10". Nail in the center of the slots and don't nail tight to the house. Keep a ¼" gap between strips, and leave space at the corners for a ½" gap between starter strips and corner posts.

Option: Install foam vinyl siding underlayment on the house using cap nails. Align the bottom of the underlayment with the starting strip. To cut panels to size, score them with a utility knife, then break them over your cutting table. Some panels need to be taped at the seams. Follow manufacturer's recommendations.

Install a corner post, keeping a ¼" gap between the top of the post and the soffit. Extend the bottom of the post ¼" below the bottom of the starter strip. Drive a nail at the top end of the uppermost slot on each side of the post (the post hangs from these nails). Make sure the post is plumb on both sides using a level. Secure the post by driving nails every 8 to 12" in the center of the slots. Do not nail the post tight. Install the other posts the same way.

4

If more than one corner post is needed to span the length of a corner, the upper post overlaps the lower post. For an outside corner post, cut off 1" from the nailing flanges on the bottom edge of the top post. For an inside corner post, cut off 1" from the nailing flange on the upper edge of the bottom post. Overlap the posts by ¾", leaving ¼" for expansion.

5

Measure and cut two J-channels that are the length of a window plus the width of the J-channel. Place one of the J-channels against the side of the window, aligning the bottom edge with the bottom edge of the window. Nail the channel in place. Nail the second J-channel against the opposite side of the window the same way.

6

At the top of the window, measure between the outside edges of the side J-channels and cut a piece of J-channel to fit. Cut a ¾" tab at each end. Bend the tabs down to form a drip edge. Miter cut the face at each end at 45°. Center the J-channel over the window and nail it in place. The top J-channel overlaps the side pieces, and the drip edges fit inside the side pieces. Do this for each window and door.

7

Measure, cut, and install J-channel along the gable ends. Nail the channels every 8 to 12". To overlap J-channels, cut 1" from the nailing hem. Overlap the channels ¾", leaving ¼" for expansion. At the gable peak, cut one channel at an angle to butt against the peak. Miter the channel on the opposite side to overlap the first channel.

(continued)

To install J-channel over a roof line, snap a chalk line along the roof flashing ½" above the roof. Align the bottom edge of the J-channel along the chalk line, and nail the channel in place. Make sure the channel does not make direct contact with the shingles.

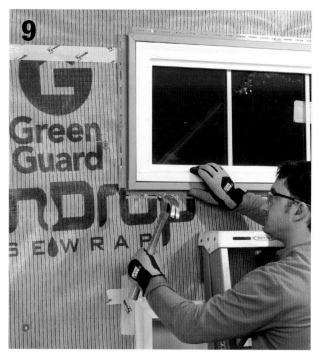

Measure, cut, and install undersill beneath each window. The undersill should be flush with the outside lip of the side channels.

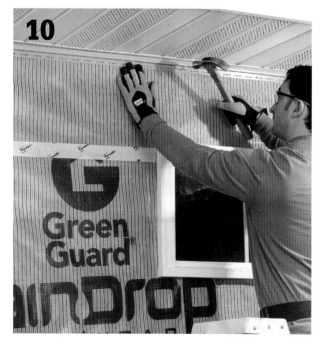

Measure, cut, and install undersill along the horizontal eaves on the house. If more than one undersill is needed, cut the nailing hem 1¼" from the end of one undersill. Overlap the undersills by 1".

Snap the locking leg on the bottom of the first panel onto the starter strip, making sure it's securely locked in place. Keep a ¼" gap between the end of the panel and the corner post. Nail the panel a minimum of every 16" on center. Don't drive the nails tight. *Note: This installation shows a vinyl siding underlayment in place.*

12

Overlap panels by 1". Cut panels so the factory cut edge is the one that's visible. Keep nails at least 6" from the end of panels to allow for smooth overlap. Do not overlap panels directly under a window.

13

Place the second row over the first, snapping the locking leg into the lock of the underlying panels. Leave ¼" gap at corners and J-channels. Install subsequent rows, staggering seams at least 24" unless separated by more than three rows. Check every several rows for level. Make adjustments in slight increments, if necessary.

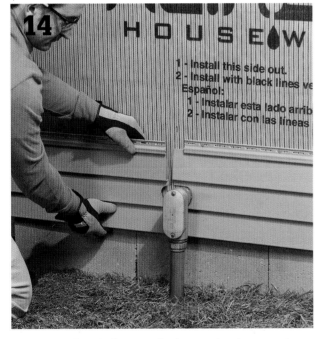

14

For hose spigots, pipes, and other protrusions, create a seam at the obstacle. Begin with a new panel to avoid extra seams. Cut an opening ¼" larger than the obstacle, planning for a 1" overlap of siding. Match the shape and contour as closely as possible. Fit the panels together around the obstruction and nail in place.

15

Place mounting blocks around outlets, lights, and doorbells. Assemble the base around the fixture, making sure it's level, and nail in place. Install siding panels, cutting them to fit around the mounting block with a ¼" gap on each side. Fasten the cover by snapping it over the block.

(continued)

16

Where panels must be notched to fit below a window, position the panel below the window and mark the edges of the window, allowing for a ¼" gap. Place a scrap piece of siding alongside the window and mark the depth of the notch, keeping a ¼" gap. Transfer the measurement to the panel, mark the notch, and cut it out. Create tabs on the outside face every 6" using a snap lock punch. Install the panel, locking the tabs into the undersill.

17

Install cut panels between windows and between windows and corners as you would regular panels. Avoid overlapping panels and creating seams in small spaces. The panels need to align with panels on the opposite side of the window.

18

To fit siding over a window, hold the panel in place over the window and mark it. Use a scrap piece of siding to mark the depth of the cut. Transfer the measurement to the full panel and cut the opening. Fit the cut edge into the J-channel above the window, lock the panel in place, and nail it.

19

For dormers, measure up from the bottom of the J-channel the height of a panel and make a mark. Measure across to the opposite J-channel. Use this measurement to mark and cut the panel to size. Cut and install panels for the rest of the dormer the same way.

20

Measure the distance between the lock on the last fully installed panel and the top of the undersill under the horizontal eaves. Subtract ¼", then mark and rip a panel to fit. Use a snap lock punch to punch tabs on the outside face every 6". Install the panel, locking the tabs into the undersill.

21

Place a scrap panel in the J-channel along the gable end of the house. Place another scrap over the last row of panels before the gable starts, slide it under the first scrap, and mark the angle where they intersect. Transfer this angle to full panels. Make a similar template for the other side. Cut the panels and set the cut edge into the J-channel, leaving a ¼" gap.

22

Cut the last piece of siding to fit the gable peak. Drive a single aluminum or stainless steel finish nail through the top of the panel to hold it in place. This is the only place where you will facenail the siding.

23

Apply caulk between all windows and J-channel, and between doors and J-channel.

Variation: How to Install Vinyl Shakes

1

Follow steps 1 to 7 on pages 120 to 121 to prepare the walls, install starter strip and corner posts, trim the doors and windows, and fasten J-channel along the gable end of the house. Install J-channel under the horizontal eaves, and use channel rather than undersill under windows.

2

Cut a straight line along the nonflanged (right) edge of the first panel using a circular saw with a carbide-tipped blade. Do not reverse the blade. If the panel has a manufacturer's mark for the cut, follow the mark. Lock the bottom of the panel over the starter strip and slide it into the corner post, keeping a ¼" gap between the panel and post.

3

Follow the exact nailing sequence prescribed by the manufacturer. For this siding, it starts with the nail slot at the top right, then the top left, then the left side flange, followed by the center of the panel. Nails are then driven every 8".

4

Fit the next panel into position over the starter strip. The nailing hem and bottom half of the panel fit over the first panel; the top shakes fit under the first panel. Overlap the panels following temperature guidelines. Nail in place using the nailing sequence.

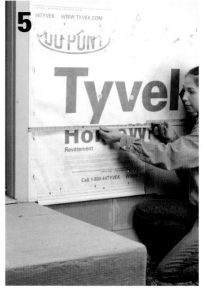

5

Install remaining panels in the row. For the last panel, measure from the correct temperature line on the last installed panel to the corner post, and subtract ¼". Cut the panel to size along the left side and install. *Tip: Vinyl shake panels must be acclimated to the outside temperature for at least an hour before installation.*

6

Alignment line

Measure from the left alignment line on the first panel of the first course to the corner post, and subtract ¼". Cut a panel to this size, removing the nonflanged edge. Place the panel over the first row, snapping the lock together and pulling up so the panel is tight. Align the left side flange with the left alignment line of the underlying panel, and nail in place.

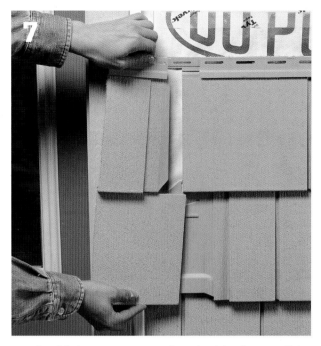

7

For the third course, measure from the right alignment line of the second panel in the second row to the corner post, and subtract ¼". Cut a panel to this size, removing the right edge. Install the panel, aligning the left side flange with the right alignment line. Install remaining rows, following step 6 for even rows and step 7 for odd rows. Cut panels to fit the opposite corner and abut doors, leaving a ¼" gap.

8

Cut panels to fit around windows, following steps 16 to 18 on page 124. Make a nail slot every 8" along the cut edge of the panels, using a nail slot punch. Set the panel in place. Drive nails through the slots at an angle. The J-channel should hide the nail heads.

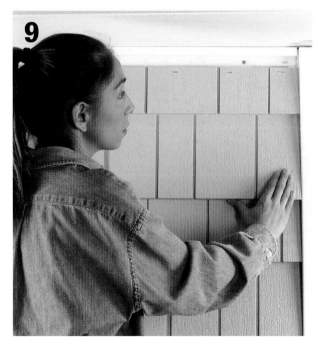

9

Measure the height for the last row of panels under the eaves, keeping a ¼" gap for movement. Rip the panels to size. Create nail slots every 8" along the cut edge. Install the panels, and nail through the slots.

Lap Siding

There are several types of horizontal board siding applications, such as clapboard, tongue and groove, bevel, and shiplap, but the most popular is lap siding, which is the project we're showing here. The installation is fairly straightforward, with each course overlapping the underlying row and covering up the nailing. We're using a measuring gauge that's preset to give each course of siding the exact same amount of overlap.

Before installing wood siding, make sure it's acclimated to your environment so it can expand or shrink prior to being nailed in place. For our project, we're using fiber-cement siding, which offers the look and texture of wood but doesn't rot or crack. The application is basically the same, although fiber cement can be more difficult to nail (you may want to predrill holes) and requires a carbide-tipped blade for cutting. Wear a respirator when cutting fiber cement since it contains silica, which can cause lung disease.

Store siding in a flat position, and keep it off the ground and covered until ready for use. When carrying the siding, make sure it doesn't bend and crack. Having a helper makes this job much easier. The siding panels need to be nailed to studs, so it's critical for the marks on the housewrap to be aligned with the wall studs. Cut the panels face down to avoid marring or damaging the faces.

If the siding is not yet primed, apply a coat of primer before installing. Also apply primer to cut edges during the installation process. Some wood and fiber-cement siding need to be painted after they're installed. Although you'll have a paint job on your hands when the project is finished, the upside is you'll have the opportunity to change the color of your siding whenever you want by applying a new coat of paint. Other sidings are available in colors that don't require painting, and the seams are caulked with a matching colored caulk.

Lap siding can be wood, fiber-cement, or one of many manufactured materials. It is easy to install and has a traditional appearance.

Tools & Materials ▸

Tape measure	Measuring gauge
Circular saw	T-bevel
Caulk gun	¼ × 1½" lath
Chalk line	Siding and trim
Paintbrush	6d corrosion-
Combination saw	resistant nails
blade (for wood)	2" corrosion-
Carbide-tipped	resistant
saw blade (for	siding nails
fiber cement)	Flexible caulk
4-ft. level	Primer

How to Install Lap Siding

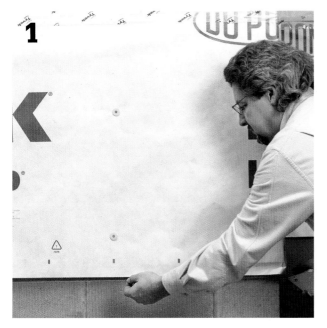

Cover the exterior walls with housewrap so the stud marks fall on the studs (see pages 116 to 117). Starting at the lowest corner of the house, snap a level line at the bottom of the wall where the siding will begin. The siding should cover the sill plate but stay above grade and concrete surfaces.

Install a corner trim board flush with the outside wall and flush with the chalk line at the bottom. Keep nails 1" from each end and ¾" from the edges. Drive two nails every 16". Overlap a second trim board on the adjacent side, aligning the edge with the face of the first board, and nail in place.

When two or more corner trim pieces are needed to complete a wall, cut a 45° bevel on the end of each board. Apply primer to the cut ends. Install the first board so the bevel faces away from the house. Place the top piece over the first board, aligning the bevels. Stagger seams between adjacent sides.

Place a corner trim board in an inside corner. Drive nails every 16".

(continued)

5

Measure and cut trim to fit around a window. Install trim along the bottom of the window first, then measure and cut trim to fit along the sides, flush with the bottom edge of the first trim piece and ⅛" above the top of the drip cap. Measure and cut trim to fit over the window, flush with the outside edges of the side trim. Drive two nails in the trim pieces every 16". Repeat for each window and door.

Option: Rather than install the trim first, wait until after the siding is in place. Then, nail the trim directly over the siding. Make sure the nails are long enough to penetrate through the siding and sheathing and into the studs by at least 1".

6

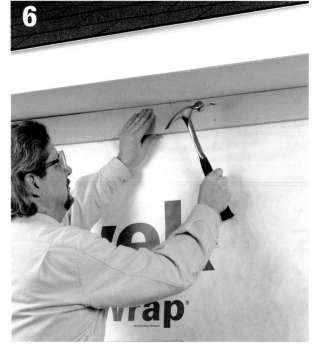

On horizontal eaves, install frieze boards directly under the soffits. Butt the frieze boards against the corner trim, and drive two nails every 16" into studs.

7

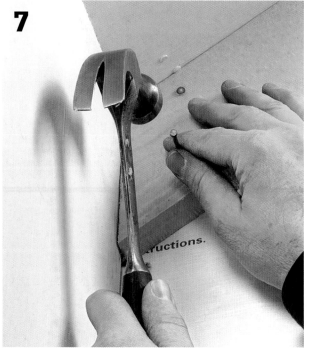

Use a T-bevel to determine the angle on the gable end of the house. Cut this angle on the end of a frieze board, and install under the soffits.

8

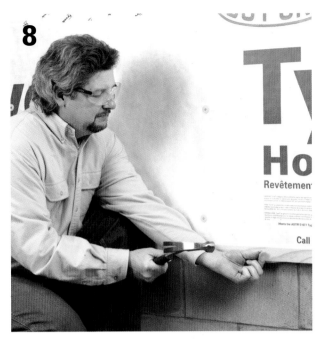

Install wood lath along the base of the walls. Align the bottom edge of the lath with the chalk line and nail in place using 6d nails. Keep the lath ⅛" from the corner trim. *Tip: Rather than buying lath, rip panels of wood or fiber-cement siding to 1½"-wide strips, and use them as lath.*

9

Cut the first siding panel so it ends halfway over a stud when the other end is placed ⅛" from a corner trim board. Apply primer to the cut end. Align the siding with the bottom edge of the lath. Keep a ⅛" gap between the siding and corner trim. Nail the panel at each stud location 1" from the top edge using siding nails.

10

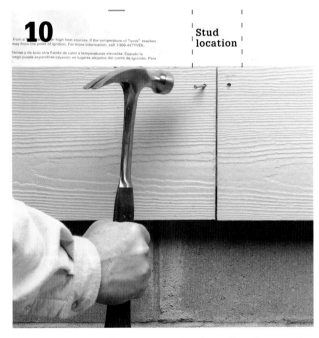

Measure and cut the next panel so it reaches the opposite corner or falls at the midpoint of a stud. Set the panel over the lath, keeping a ⅛" gap between the first panel and the second panel. Nail the panel ⅜" from the seam edge and at every stud.

11

Set the measuring gauge (inset photo) to give the panels a minimum of 1¼" overlap. Place the second row of panels over the first, using the measuring gauge to set the amount of overlap. Offset seams by at least one stud. Repeat this procedure for subsequent rows. Check every five or six rows for level. Make adjustments in small increments. Cut or notch panels as necessary to fit around protrusions in the walls.

(continued)

12

For windows, slide the siding panel against the bottom window trim. Mark the panel ⅛" from the outside edges of the side trim. Place a scrap piece of siding next to the window trim at the proper overlap. Mark the depth of the cut ⅛" below the bottom trim. Transfer the measurement to the siding panel and cut it to fit. Install the cutout panel around the window. Do the same at the top of the window.

Option: Siding 12" or wider, or siding nailed 24" on center, needs to be facenailed. The siding is overlapped a minimum of 1¼" and nailed ¾ to 1" from the bottom. Drive the nail through both planks of siding into the stud using corrosion-resistant siding nails.

13

When installing the siding over a roof line, keep the panels 1 to 2" above the roofing. Use a T-bevel to determine the angle of the roof line, and transfer the angle to the siding. Cut the panels to fit. Place the bottom edge of the siding over the roof flashing, and nail the panel in place.

14

Frieze

Rip the last row of panels to fit ⅛" below the frieze boards under the horizontal eaves. Nail the panels in place.

15

Use a T-bevel to determine the angle of the roof line on the gable ends of the house. Transfer the angle to the panels, and cut them to fit.

16

Keep the panels ⅛" from the rake boards, and nail them in place along the gable end.

17

Fill all gaps between panels and trim with flexible, paintable caulk. Paint the siding as desired (see Painting & Staining Siding, beginning on page 211).

Wood Shakes & Shingles

The siding application for shakes and for shingles is basically the same, but there is a difference between the two materials. Shakes are hand split then sawn in half, giving them a rough surface and a flat, smooth back. Shingles are machine sawn on both sides and sanded to create smooth, tapered boards that are thinner than shakes. Both shakes and shingles are typically made from cedar.

Shakes and shingles are usually installed in a pattern called single coursing, which is what's used for our project. Each piece of siding overlaps the one below. For a greater look of depth, consider the double course or staggered butt course shown on the opposite page. Likewise, there is more than one way to treat corners, with alternatives featured on the opposite page. The more overlap you have between rows, the more protection the siding provides, although it also consumes more siding materials.

Each shake or shingle is installed with two corrosion-resistant nails, most commonly 4d to 7d nails. The nail size is determined by the size and type of shake or shingle. Check manufacturer's recommendations. The manufacturer will also specify the spacing between siding pieces. Most shakes and shingles will expand after installation, although some that are green or freshly cut may actually shrink.

The siding must be installed over sheathing that has a solid nailing surface, such as plywood. If there isn't a suitable nailing surface, install 1 × 3 or 1 × 4 furring strips across the house for nailing. Felt paper is commonly used as an underlayment, but check building codes for underlayment requirements in your area.

Tools & Materials ▸

Hammer	Chalk gun
Handsaw	Shakes or shingles
or coping saw	Cedar trim boards
Tape measure	(2 × 2, 1 × 3,
Utility knife	1 × 4)
Stapler	Nails
Chalk line	30# felt paper
Line level	Staples
Paintbrush	Sealer
T-bevel	Flexible caulk

Wood shakes and shingles are commonly used as siding for Victorian and Cape Cod-style houses, although they can be used on any type of house to create a rustic look.

Variations for Coursing

Double-course installation offers a greater look of depth between rows. Each course of shingles is installed ½" lower than an undercourse that's placed beneath it. A lower-grade, less-expensive shingle is typically used for the undercourse.

Staggered butt–course installation features a random, three-dimensional look. The application starts with a double starter row, and shingles in overlapping courses are staggered by up to 1".

Variations for Corner Installations

Woven corners have shingles that overlap at the corners for a weave effect. This overlap alternates between walls with each successive course.

Mitered corners are made by cutting corner shingles at a 45° angle and butting them together. This method is very time-consuming.

How to Install Single-course Wood Shakes & Shingles

Cover the exterior sheathing with felt paper. Starting at the bottom of a wall, install the paper horizontally using staples. Wrap corners a minimum of 4". Overlap vertical seams 6" and horizontal seams 2". Cut out openings around doors and windows.

Starting at the lowest corner of the house, snap a level chalk line at the bottom of each wall where the siding will start. Measure the height of the wall from the chalk line to the soffits.

To determine the exposure of the shingles—the amount of wood revealed beneath the overlap—divide the wall height by the number of proposed rows. The goal is to find an exposure measurement that can be multiplied by a whole number to equal the wall height—a 120" wall can have twelve rows with a 10" exposure, for example. Create a story pole on a straight 1 × 3 by making a series of marks equal to the exposure. *Tip: It's best for rows to align with the tops and bottoms of doors and windows.*

Place the story pole at a corner, aligning the bottom with the chalk line. Transfer the marks onto the wall. Do this at each corner, door, and window location.

Place a 1 × 3 board at an outside corner, aligning it with the chalk line at the bottom. Keep the outside edge flush with the adjacent wall. Nail it in place. Overlap the edge of the board with a 1 × 4, align it with the chalk line, and nail in place. If more than one trim board is needed to span the length of the wall, miter the ends at 45° and place them together. Do this for all outside corners. *Tip: As soon as you cut a shingle or piece of trim, apply sealer to the cut edge.*

Fasten a 2 × 2 in an inside corner flush with the chalk line at the bottom. If more than one board is needed to span the height of the wall, miter the adjoining ends at 45° and butt them together.

If the chalk line is hard to see, run a string from the bottom of the corner trim pieces. Starting at a corner, install the starter row of shingles ½" above the chalk line. Keep the manufacturer's recommended distance between shingles and between shingles and trim, usually a ⅛ to ¼" gap. Keep nails ¾" from edges and 1" above the line of exposure.

Place the first course of shingles over the starter row flush with the chalk line at the bottom. Overlap the seams in the starter course by at least 1½".

(continued)

Snap a chalk line across the shingles to mark the exposure using the reference lines from step 4. Install a course of shingles at the chalk line, offsetting the seams. Install remaining rows the same way.

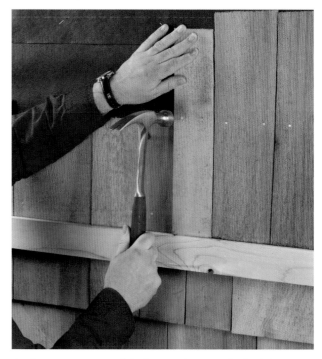

Option: To ensure straight lines, tack a 1 × 4 flush with your reference lines. Nail the board through gaps between shingles. Use the board as a guide for installing the shingles.

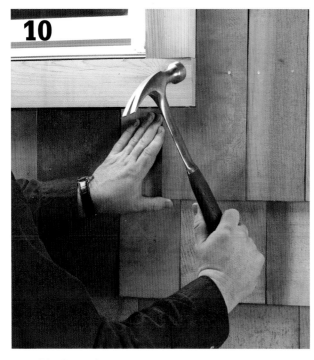

Cut shingles to fit around doors, windows, and protrusions in the walls using a coping saw or handsaw. Make sure gaps between shingles aren't aligned with the edges of doors and windows. *Tip: Whenever possible, plan your layout so you can install full shingles next to doors and windows rather than cutting shingles to fit.*

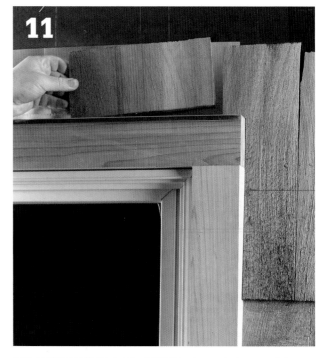

Cut and install the tops of shingles over windows and doors. Align the tops with adjacent shingles on either side of the door or window.

12

When applying shingles on a dormer or above a roof line, keep the bottom edge of the shingles ½" above the roof shingles. Cut shingles with a handsaw or circular saw.

13

Measure and cut the last row of shingles to fit under the horizontal eaves. Leave the recommended gap between shingles and soffits. Nail the shingles in place.

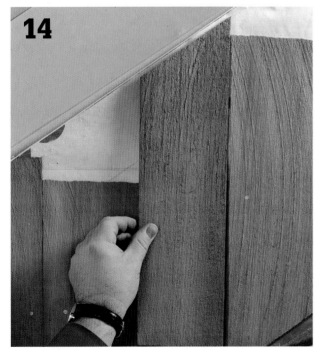

14

Use a T-bevel to determine the roof angle on the gable end of the house. Cut shingles at this angle for each row at the gable end using a handsaw or circular saw. Install shingles up to the peak. *Tip: As you near the top of a wall, measure from the soffits to the shingles on each side of the wall. If the measurements aren't equal, make small adjustments in successive rows until the distance is the same.*

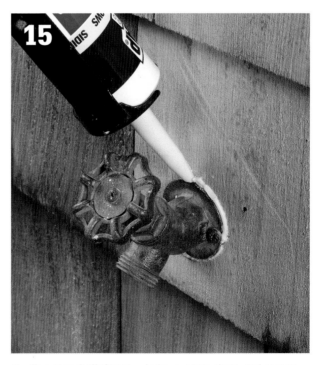

15

Caulk around all doors, windows, protrusions, and corner trim. Apply your choice of stain or primer and paint (see Painting & Staining Siding, starting on page 211).

Board & Batten Siding

Board and batten is a vertically installed siding that offers a rustic look and makes houses appear taller. The application consists of installing wide boards vertically on the walls, then placing narrow boards called battens over the seams.

Although there are no set board and batten widths, a popular combination is 1 × 10" boards with 1 × 3" battens, which is what we're using for this project. Our lumber is knotty cedar, which is often used for board and batten applications.

Regardless of the type and size of lumber you choose, the battens need to overlap the boards by at least ½". To maintain a uniform look, measure the length of the wall, and the width of the boards, and determine the appropriate spacing between boards so you can install a full board at the end of the wall. Ripping the last board to fit will ruin the symmetry you've established.

Before installing the siding, you'll need to install horizontal blocking lines or furring strips on the walls. This gives you a firm nailing base for the siding. Nails must be driven 1½" into solid wood. Nailing directly to your sheathing, even if it's plywood, will not provide sufficient hold. Because the nailing strips add thickness to your walls, you'll need to extend the jambs and sills around your doors and windows.

Another way to achieve the board-on-board look is to use board and batten panels (page 145). These panels feature a reverse batten style, in which the batten is placed behind the simulated boards. The panels are typically available in 4 × 8- or 4 × 9-foot sheets to span the length of the wall. Be sure to purchase panels that are rated for exterior use.

Tools & Materials ▸

Tape measure	4-ft. level
Circular saw	Paintbrush
Hammer	Cedar lumber (1 × 10, 1 × 3)
Chalk line	1 × 3 nailing strips
Line level	2 × 4
Pry bar	8d and 10d corrosion-
Tin snips	resistant box nails
Level	Drip caps
Jigsaw	6d galvanized box nails
T-bevel	Sealer
Caulk gun	Caulk

The board and batten siding on the second level offers vertical, parallel lines that are juxtaposed against the horizontal siding on the lower level. The effect is a contrasting exterior that uses multiple colors.

How to Install Board & Batten Siding

1

Cover the walls with housewrap (pages 116 to 117). Starting at the bottom of the wall, fasten horizontal nailing strips every 16 to 24". Nail the strips to studs using 8d nails. Install nailing strips around all doors and windows. Do this for each wall.

2

Carefully remove the exterior trim around windows and doors using a pry bar. Rip jamb extenders to the same width as the jambs. *Tip: Jamb extenders should be thick enough to be flush with the outside of the board siding when installed.*

3

Cut an extender to fit over a window. Nail it in place using nails that penetrate the jamb by at least 1". Cut and install jambs along the sides of the window, then do the same for the sill. Apply sealer to all cut edges.

4

Cut a piece of drip cap to size to fit over the window using tin snips. Set the drip cap in place so the bottom lip is over the jamb extension. Nail the drip cap in the upper corners using 6d galvanized nails. Repeat steps 2 to 4 for each window and door.

(continued)

5

Install ledger here

Starting at a corner, snap a level chalk line at the bottom of the wall where you want to start the siding. Make sure it's below the nailing strips. Install a straight 2 × 4 flush with the chalk line to use as a temporary ledger. *Tip: Don't cut all boards to size at the start of a wall. The distance from the ledger to the soffits can change, which can impact the length of the boards.*

6

Measure from the ledger to the soffits, then subtract ⅛". Cut a siding board to this length. Set the bottom of the board on the ledger and align the side with the edge of the wall. For boards 6" and narrower, drive one 8d nail in the center at each nailing strip. For boards wider than 6", drive two nails 3" apart.

7

Wood spacer

Nail "handle" for spacer removal

Cut the next board to size and set in place on the ledger. Keep your predetermined gap between boards, but make sure the batten will overlap each board by at least ½". Nail in place at each nailing strip. Install remaining boards the same way. Check every few boards with a level to make sure they're plumb. If they're not, adjust slightly until plumb. To maintain even spacing between boards, cut wood spacers the size of your gaps and use them when installing each board.

8

At window locations, set a board next to the window, keeping the bottom on the ledger. Mark the board ⅛" above and below the outside of the top and bottom jambs.

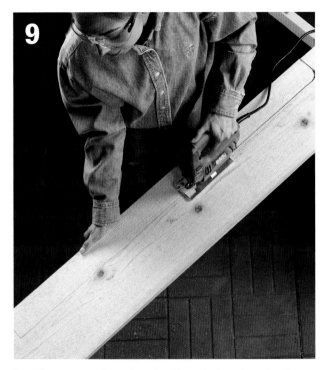

9

Position a scrap board under the window, keeping the proper gap from the last installed board. Mark the scrap board ⅛" past the outside edge of the side jamb. Use this measurement to mark the cutout on the board you marked in step 8. Cut out the window opening using a jigsaw.

10

Set the board in place, keeping a ⅛" gap around the window jamb. When installing, drive only one nail per nailing strip in the area next to the window. Repeat steps 8 to 10 for each window and door.

11

If more than one board is needed to span the height of a wall, cut a 45° bevel in the ends of the adjoining boards and butt them together. Make sure the seam falls over a nailing strip. Offset seams by at least one nailing strip.

12

When starting a new wall, place the first board over the edge of the last installed board on the adjacent wall. Nail the board in place.

(continued)

13

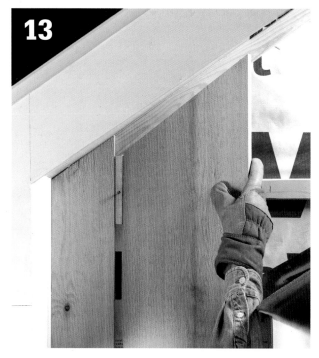

At the gable end of the house, use a T-bevel to determine the pitch of the roof. Transfer the angle to the boards, cut to size, and install. The length of each board needs to be measured individually since the distance changes along the gable end.

14

Fill gaps between the boards and soffits, and between the boards and jambs with flexible, paintable caulk.

15

Measure and cut battens to size. Center a batten over each gap between boards. Drive one 10d nail in the battens at each nailing strip. Once the battens are installed, remove the ledger board. Paint the siding (see Painting & Staining Siding, starting on page 211).

Variation: To create a deep channel look, install the battens first, then place the boards over the battens.

How to Install Board & Batten Paneling

1

2

3

Cover the walls with housewrap (pages 116 to 117). Snap a level line at the base of the wall where the siding will start. Install a straight ledger board flush with the line, following step 5 on page 142.

Starting at a corner, measure from the ledger to the soffits, subtract ⅛", and cut the panel to size. Place the panel on the ledger flush with the corner and install using corrosion-resistant nails that penetrate studs by 1½".

If the panels have built-in shiplaps, overlap the panels as specified by the manufacturer. If the panels don't have laps, leave ⅛" gaps between panels.

4

5

Place a panel next to a window and make a mark ⅛" above and below the outside of the jambs. Set a scrap piece in place under the window and make a mark ⅛" past the side jambs. Transfer the measurements to the panel, then cut out the window opening using a jigsaw. Do the same for each door, window, and protrusion.

Follow steps 13 and 14 on page 144 to cut panels to fit the gable end of the house and to caulk between panels and soffits. To create a more finished look, install 1 × 3 or 1 × 4 trim around doors, windows, corners, and under soffits. Paint the siding (see Painting & Staining Siding, starting on page 211).

Log Cabin Siding

Log cabin siding is an inexpensive way to achieve the rustic look of log homes. Since the siding is not composed of full logs, it uses less wood, making it less expensive than traditional log cabins. But from the outside, it's almost impossible to tell that the house is not an actual log cabin. The log-tail corners complete the authentic appearance. Where the log tails would restrict a pathway or entrance, or create a design problem, vertical log corners can be used.

Log cabin siding is generally available in cedar or pine. For our project, we're using 2 × 8 pine siding, which is considerably less expensive than cedar. The siding is facenailed, but the nails are hardly visible. To speed up installation, rent an air compressor and nail gun. If you choose to hand nail, be sure to use a hammer with a smooth face. A corrugated face could mar the siding.

You can cut the siding with a circular saw, but a compound saw or miter saw works better. It's critical for the cuts to be square since the siding pieces butt against each other. The siding must be nailed to studs, so be sure the stud marks on the housewrap are properly aligned with the studs in the walls.

Tools & Materials ▸

Hammer
Level
Chalk line
Chisel
Tape measure
Drill
4-ft. level
Caulk gun
Jigsaw
Miter saw or sliding
   compound saw
T-bevel
Paintbrush
Log cabin siding
Cedar or pine
   (2 × 2s, 2 × 4s,
   2 × 6s)
Housewrap
Cap nails
Left- and right-
   side corners
Hot-dipped
   galvanized siding
   nails (12d or 16d)
Polyurethane caulk
Sealer

This house isn't really a log cabin, but you'd never know it from the outside. The log cabin siding provides the charm and realism of an actual log home.

How to Install Log Cabin Siding

Cover the walls with housewrap (pages 116 to 117) and snap a level line around the base of the walls for the first row of siding following step 1 on page 129. Place a 2 × 2 in each inside corner flush with the chalk line at the bottom, and nail in place. If more than one 2 × 2 is needed to span the wall, cut a 45° bevel at the joining ends.

Use 2 × 2s or 2 × 4s to trim doors and windows. Measure the top, bottom, and sides of doors and windows, add ¼" to each piece, and cut to size. Install the trim, keeping a ⅛" gap between the window and door frames and the trim.

Apply 2 × 2 trim around electrical outlets, the electric meter, and vents.

Option: If using vertical corners, place the corner on the wall flush with the chalk line at the bottom, and nail in place. Install vertical corners before applying any siding. Keep siding ⅛" from these corners.

(continued)

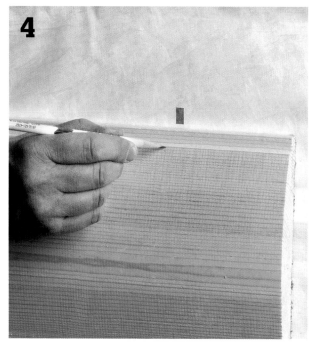

4

Hold a piece of siding in place with the bottom (groove) edge aligned with the chalk line (step 1) and the end flush with an outside corner. Mark the opposite end at the midpoint of the last stud it crosses. Cut the siding at the mark. Apply sealer to the cut end. *Tip: Apply sealer to the cut ends of siding, trim, and corners before installing.*

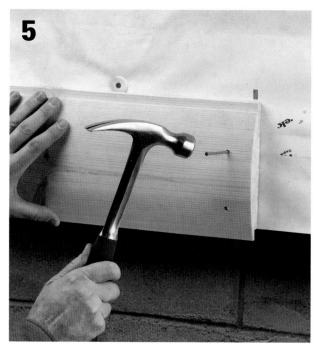

5

Set the siding back in place along the chalk line flush with the corner. Fasten it to the wall with two siding nails at each stud location. Drive the first nail 1½" from the bottom edge, and the second nail 3 to 4" above that. Cut the next piece to reach the opposite corner, butt it against the first piece, and install.

6

On the adjacent wall, start with a corner piece. Hold it in place so the log tail overlaps the adjacent siding. Mark the opposite end at the last stud. Cut it to length, set it along the chalk line so the corner overlaps the adjacent wall, and nail in place. Install the remaining first course the same way.

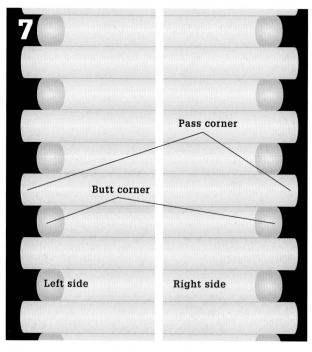

7

Alternate between the butt and the pass at the corners for each row of siding. The corners at both ends of a wall must be the same, either both butts or both passes, for each course. You cannot have a butt at one end of the wall and a pass at the opposite corner.

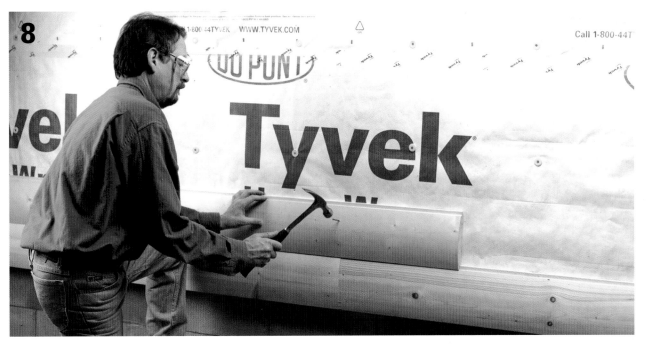

8

Place the second row of siding over the first, setting the groove over the lip of the siding below. Offset joints between rows by at least two studs. Keep a ⅛" gap between the siding and inside corners. Install remaining courses the same way. *Tip: There are left-side and right-side corner pieces. Be sure to use the correct piece for each corner. Start the siding on a wall that has a "butt" corner, then overlap it with a "pass" on the adjacent side. For a butt corner, the end of the siding is flush with the corner. A pass corner extends past the corner to overlap siding on the adjacent wall.*

9

For hose spigots and other small wall protrusions that you don't frame around, drill a hole in the siding at the proper location, then place the siding over the object. To keep the hole as small as possible, you may need to remove the protrusion, then reinsert it after the siding is in place.

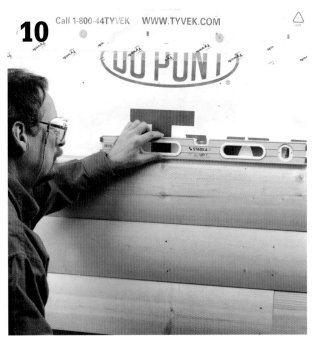

10

Check every few rows of siding with a level. If necessary, leave a small gap between the grooves and lips in the siding until the rows are level. Make the changes subtly over several courses. *Tip: Start with 8-ft. sections of log-tail corner pieces for the first row. With each successive course, move the joints over two studs until you can use 4-ft. sections, then start again with 8-ft. pieces.*

(continued)

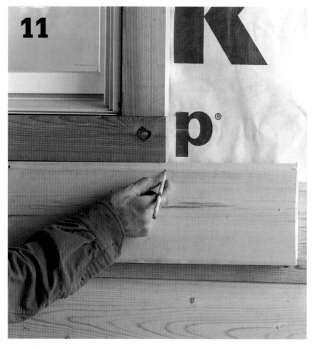

11

Install siding up to the bottom of windows. Hold a piece of siding in place below the window framing. Make a mark on the siding ⅛" past the outside edge of the side window trim. Place a scrap of siding next to the window over the last installed row. Mark the siding piece ⅛" below the edge of the window.

12

Transfer the measurements from the last step to a piece of siding. Cut out the opening using a jigsaw.

13

Install the siding, keeping a ⅛" gap around the window frame. As you continue installing rows of siding, maintain a ⅛" gap between the siding and trim.

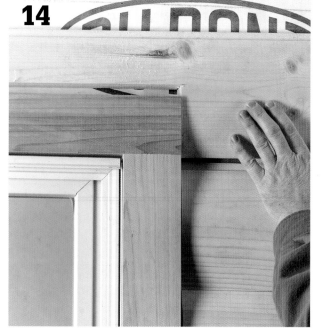

14

Follow steps 11 to 12 to mark and cut siding to fit over the top of doors and windows. Center the siding opening over the door and window, and nail in place. *Tip: For best appearance, keep joints in the siding from falling directly above or below windows and doors.*

15

At light fixture locations, drill a hole in the siding for electrical wires. To make a flat surface to hold the fixture, start at the wire hole and work out 2¾" on each side, making a series of 1"-deep cuts in the siding. Chisel out the wood until the surface is flat, and apply sealer. Install the siding, feeding the wires through the hole. Cut a 2 × 6 the height of the siding, drill a hole for the wiring, and install in the notch. Mount the fixture on the 2 × 6.

16

For the top row, measure the distance from the bottom of the lip of the last installed row of siding to the eaves. Subtract ⅛" and rip siding to this measurement. Nail the siding in place under the eaves.

17

On the gable ends of the house, use a T-bevel to determine the roof angle. Cut the ends of the siding at this angle, then install along the gable.

18

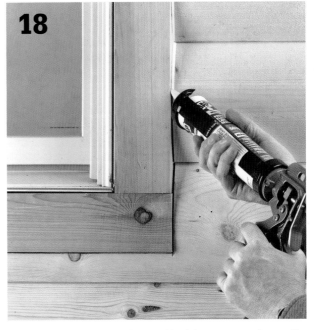

Caulk between the siding and inside corners. Also caulk between siding and vertical corners, siding and window and door framing, and around wall protrusions. Do not apply caulk to the joints between siding. Stain the siding following the instructions that start on page 230.

Finishing Walls with Masonry

The thought of hefting heavy rock or mixing batch after batch of stucco mix may sound like miserable work for those who have never tried a masonry project, but in reality masonry isn't as difficult as it may seem. In fact, all it may take is a dash of brick or veneered stone here and there to give your home the charm that masonry can bring, without much work at all. Granted, coating every wall with stucco is a big job that's better left to those who make a living doing it, but don't be afraid to try your hand at it. With a small collection of masonry tools and maybe a rented mixer, you'll have what you need to tackle the job yourself. This chapter will walk you through the process of completing five different masonry projects. One of them requires no mortar at all.

As with any roofing or siding project, make sure to correctly prepare walls before you begin the job. Proper wrapping, flashing, and structural reinforcement will impact how long and well your masonry project stands the test of time.

In this chapter:

- Masonry Tools & Materials
- Brick
- Veneer Stone
- Mortarless Brick Veneer
- Stucco
- Cement

Masonry Tools & Materials

Layout and measuring tools for preparing job sites and installing and levelling concrete forms include a 2-ft. level (A), a 4-ft. level (B), and a tape measure (C).

Other useful tools are a chalk line (A), a carpenter's square (B), a stud finder (C), a laser level (D).

Safety tools and equipment include particle masks, gloves, safety glasses, and tall rubber boots. Wear protective gear when handling dry or mixed concrete. These mixes are very alkaline and can burn eyes and skin.

Mixing and pouring tools include masonry hoe and mortar box for mixing small amounts of concrete; garden hose and bucket for delivering and measuring water; and power mixer for mixing medium-sized loads of concrete.

Using the right tools for your masonry projects make the job much easier and will save a lot of time. The most common tools for masonry siding projects such as brick, stone, and stucco are as follows: mortar bag (A) for applying clean lines of mortar and grout; inside corner tool (B) for shaping and siding inside corners of concrete; outside corner tool (C) for shaping and forming outside corners of concrete; whisk broom (D) for applying different finishes and textures to concrete; mortar hawk (E), also known as mortarboard, for holding mortar while laying brick, block, or stone; wood flat (F) for flat application of latex or stucco; jointing tools (G, H, I, J), also known as jointers, for forming joints in brick, block, or stone are available in different sizes and shapes to match your specific joint width; wide-mouth nippers (K) for cutting stone; aviation snips (L) for cutting stucco lath; groover (M) for forming joints in concrete slabs or treads in steps; edger (N) for shaping and forming concrete edges; mason's hammer (O) for setting or cutting brick, block, or stone; mason's trowel (P) for mixing and moving mortar; hand maul (Q) for breaking up concrete and tapping bricks or stone into place in mortar; square-end trowel (R) for pressing mortar into lath.

Brick

Brick veneer is essentially a brick wall built around the exterior walls of a house. It's attached to the house with metal wall ties and supported by a metal shelf hanger on the foundation. It's best to use queen-sized bricks for veneer projects because they're thinner than standard construction bricks. This means less weight for the house walls to support. Even so, brick veneer is quite heavy. Ask your local building inspector about building code rules that apply to your project. In the project shown here, brick veneer is installed over the foundation walls and side walls up to the bottom of the windowsills on the first floor of the house. The siding materials in these areas are removed before installing the brick.

Construct a story pole before you start laying the brick so you can check your work as you go along to be sure your mortar joints are of a consistent thickness. A standard ⅜" gap is used in the project shown here.

Tools & Materials ▸

Hammer	30 mil PVC
Circular saw	roll flashing
Combination square	Corrugated metal
Level	wall ties
Drill with masonry bit	Brickmold for
Socket wrench set	sill extensions
Staple gun	Sill-nosing trim
Mason's trowel	Type N mortar
Masonry hoe	Bricks
Mortar box	⅜-dia. cotton rope
Mason's chisel	
Maul	
Pressure-treated	
2 × 4s	
⅜ × 4" lag screws	
and washers	
2 × 2	
Lead sleeve anchors	
Angle iron for metal	
shelf supports	

Labels: Windowsill · Sill extension · Rowlock brick · Field bricks · ½" gap · Building paper · Sheathing · Corrugated wall tie · Weep-hole rope · PVC flashing · Ground level · Metal shelf hanger · Foundation wall · Rim joist · Sill plate

Anatomy of a brick veneer facade: Queen-sized bricks are stacked onto a metal or concrete shelf and connected to the foundation and walls with metal ties. Rowlock bricks are cut to follow the slope of the windowsills, then laid on edge over the top course of bricks.

How to Install Brick Veneer

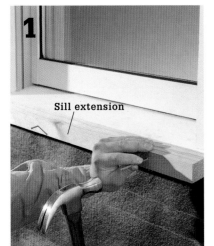

Remove all siding materials in the area you plan to finish with brick veneer. Before laying out the project, cut the sill extension from a pressure-treated 2 × 4. Tack the extension to the sill temporarily.

Precut the bricks to follow the slope of the sill and overhang the field brick by 2". Position this rowlock brick directly under the sill extension. Use a combination square or level to transfer the lowest point on the brick onto the sheathing (marking the height for the top course of brick in the field). Use a level to extend the line. Remove the sill extensions.

Make a story pole long enough to span the project area. Mark the pole with ⅜" joints between bricks. Dig a 12"-wide, 12"-deep trench next to the wall. Position the pole so the top-course line on the sheathing aligns with a top mark for a brick on the pole. Mark a line for the first course on the wall below ground level.

Extend the mark for the first-course height across the foundation wall using a level as a guide. Measure the thickness of the metal shelf (usually ¼") and drill pilot holes for 10d nails into the foundation at 16" intervals along the first-course line, far enough below the line to allow for the thickness of the shelf. Slip nails into the pilot holes to create temporary support for the shelf.

Set the metal shelf onto the temporary supports. Mark the location of the center web of each block onto the vertical face of the shelf. Remove the shelf and drill ⅜"-dia. holes for lag screws at the web marks. Set the shelf back onto the temporary supports and outline the predrilled holes on the blocks. Remove the shelf and drill holes for the masonry anchors into the foundation using a masonry bit. Drive masonry anchors into the holes.

(continued)

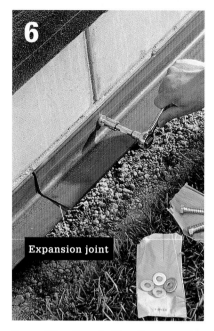

6

Expansion joint

Reposition the shelf on the supports so the predrilled holes align with the masonry anchors. Attach the shelf to the foundation wall with ⅜ × 4" lag screws and washers. Allow ¹⁄₁₆" for an expansion joint between shelf sections. Remove the temporary support nails.

7

After all sections of the metal shelf are attached, staple 30 mil PVC flashing above the foundation wall so it overlaps the metal shelf.

8

Test-fit the first course on the shelf. Work in from the ends using spacers to set the gaps between bricks. You may need to cut the final brick for the course (see page 160). Or, choose a pattern such as running bond that uses cut bricks.

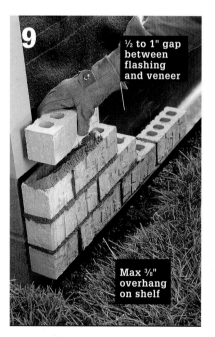

9

½ to 1" gap between flashing and veneer

Max ⅜" overhang on shelf

Build up the corners two courses above ground level, then attach line blocks and mason's string to the end bricks. Fill in the field bricks so they align with the strings. Every 30 minutes, smooth mortar joints that are firm.

10

Attach another course of PVC flashing to the wall so it covers the top course of bricks, then staple building paper to the wall so it overlaps the top edge of the PVC flashing by at least 12". Mark wall-stud locations on the building paper.

11

Use the story pole to mark layout lines for the tops of every fifth course of bricks. Attach corrugated metal wall ties to the sheathing where the brick lines meet the marked wall-stud locations.

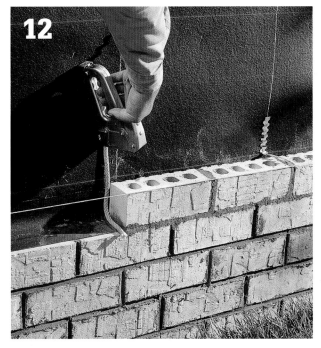

Fill in the next course of bricks, applying mortar directly onto the PVC flashing. At every third mortar joint in this course, tack a 10" piece of ⅜"-dia. cotton rope to the sheathing so it extends all the way through the bottom of the joint, creating a weep hole for drainage. Embed the metal wall ties in the mortar beds applied to this course.

Add courses of bricks, building up corners first, then filling in the field. Embed the wall ties into the mortar beds as you reach them. Use corner blocks and a mason's string to verify the alignment, and check frequently with a 4-ft. level to make sure the veneer is plumb.

Apply a ½"-thick mortar bed to the top course and begin laying the rowlock bricks with the cut ends against the wall. Apply a layer of mortar to the bottom of each rowlock brick, then press the brick up against the sheathing with the top edge following the slope of the windowsills.

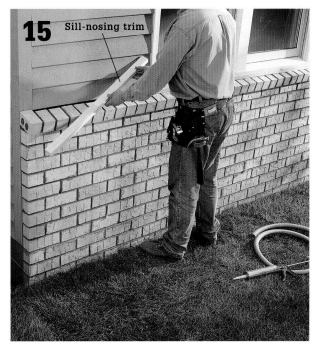

Sill-nosing trim

Finish-nail the sill extensions (step 1, page 157) to the windowsills. Nail sill-nosing trim to the siding to cover any gaps above the rowlock course. Fill cores of exposed rowlock blocks with mortar, and caulk any gaps around the veneer with silicone caulk.

HOW TO SCORE & CUT BRICK

Score all four sides of the brick first with a brickset chisel and maul when cuts fall over the web area, and not over the core. Tap the chisel to leave scored cutting marks ⅛ to ¼" deep, then strike a firm final blow to the chisel to split the brick. Properly scored bricks split cleanly with one firm blow.

Option: When you need to split a lot of bricks uniformly and quickly, use a circular saw fitted with a masonry blade to score the bricks, then split them individually with a chisel. For quick scoring, clamp them securely at each end with a pipe or bar clamp, making sure the ends are aligned. Remember: Wear eye protection when using striking or cutting tools, as well as a respirator to protect your lungs from the dust.

HOW TO ANGLE-CUT BRICK

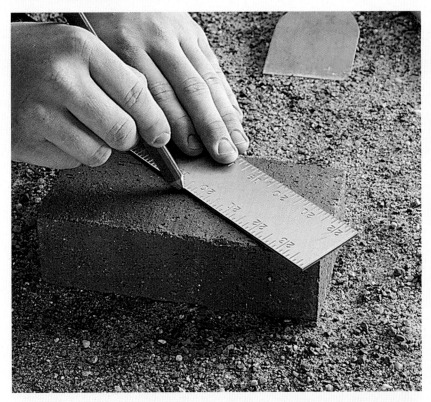

Mark the final cutting line on the brick. To avoid ruining the brick, you will need to make gradual cuts until you reach this line. Score a straight line for the first cut in the waste area of the brick about ⅛" from the starting point of the final cutting line, perpendicular to the edge of the brick. Make the first cut.

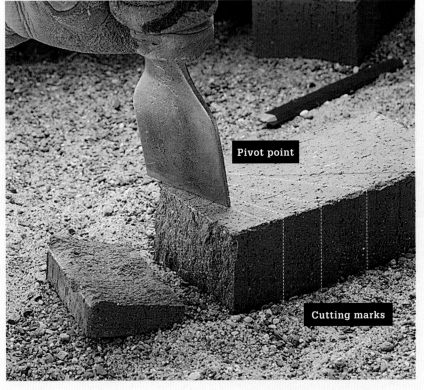

Pivot point

Cutting marks

Keep the chisel stationary at the point of the first cut, pivot it slightly, then score and cut again. It is important to keep the pivot point of the chisel at the edge of the brick. Repeat until all of the waste area is removed.

Veneer Stone

If you want the look of stone on your house without the rigors of cutting and moving heavy materials, veneer stone is ideal. Two types of veneer are available. One is natural stone that has been cut into thin pieces designed for finishing walls, hearths, and other surfaces. The other is made from concrete that's molded and tinted to look like natural stone, but it's even lighter and easier to apply to these surfaces.

Whether you use natural or manufactured veneer, wet each stone, then apply mortar to the back before pressing it onto the mortared wall. Wetting and mortaring a stone (called parging) results in maximum adhesion between the stone and the wall. The challenge is to arrange the stones so that large and small stones and various hues and shapes alternate across the span of the wall.

This project is designed for installing veneer stone over plywood sheathing, which has the strength to support layers of building paper, lath, and veneer. If your walls are covered with fiberboard or any other type of sheathing, ask the veneer manufacturer for recommendations. Here, we used materials from Cultured Stone Corporation (see Resourcces).

Tools & Materials ▸

Hammer
  or staple gun
Drill
Wheelbarrow
Hoe
Square-end trowel
Circular saw
Wide-mouth nippers
  or mason's
  hammer
Dust mask
Level
Jointing tool
Mortar bag
Spray bottle
Whisk broom
Type M mortar mix
Mortar tint
  (optional)

Expanded galvanized
  metal lath
1½" (minimum)
  galvanized
  roofing nails or
  heavy-duty staples
2 × 4 lumber
15# building paper

Find the square footage of veneer stone required for your project by multiplying the length by the height of the area. Subtract the square footage of window and door openings and corner pieces. One lin. ft. of corner pieces covers approximately three-quarters of a sq. ft. of flat area, so you can reduce the square footage of flat stone required by ¾ sq. ft. for each lin. ft. of inside or outside corner. It's best to increase your estimate by 5 to 10 percent to allow for trimming.

How to Finish Walls with Stone Veneer

1 Cover the wall with building paper, overlapping seams by 4". Nail or staple lath every 6" into the wall studs and midway between studs. Nails or staples should penetrate 1" into the studs. Paper and lath must extend at least 16" around corners where veneer is installed.

2 Stake a level 2 × 4 against the foundation as a temporary ledger to keep the bottom edge of the veneer 4" above grade. The gap between the bottom course and the ground will reduce staining of the veneer by plants and soil.

3 Spread out the materials on the ground so you can select pieces of varying size, shape, and color, and create contrast in the overall appearance. Alternate the use of large and small, heavily textured and smooth, and thick and thin pieces.

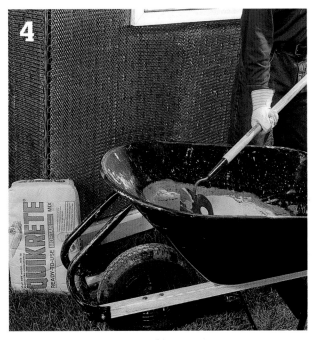

4 Mix a batch of Type M mortar that's firm but still moist. Mortar that's too dry or too wet is hard to work with and may fail to bond properly.

(continued)

Use a square-end trowel to press a ½ to ¾" layer of mortar into the lath. To ensure that mortar doesn't set up too quickly, start with a 5-sq.-ft. area. Once you determine your pace, you can mortar larger areas. *Tip: Mix in small amounts of water to retemper mortar that has begun to thicken.*

Install corner pieces first, alternating long and short legs. Wet and parge each piece, then press it firmly against the freshly mortared wall so some mortar squeezes out. Joints between stones should be no wider than ½" and should remain as consistent as possible across the wall.

Once the corner pieces are in place, install flat pieces working from the corner toward the center of the wall.

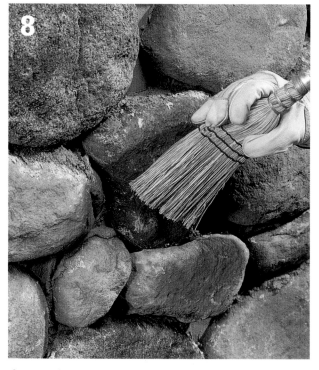

If mortar becomes smeared on a stone, remove it with a whisk broom or soft-bristle brush after the mortar has begun to dry. Never use a wire brush or a wet brush of any kind.

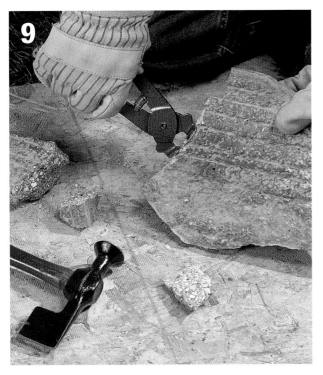

9

Use wide-mouth nippers or a mason's hammer to trim and shape pieces to fit. Do your best to limit trimming so each piece retains its natural look.

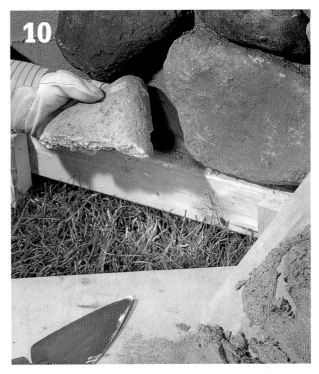

10

You can hide cut edges that are well above or below eye level simply by rotating a stone. If an edge remains visible, use mortar to cover. Let the mortar cure for 24 hours, then remove the 2 × 4 and stakes, taking care not to dislodge any stones.

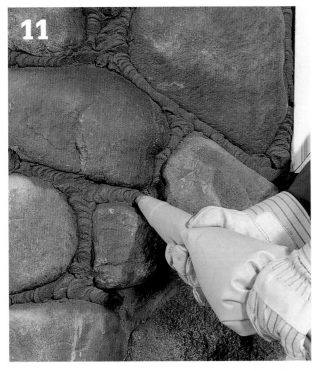

11

Once the wall is covered in veneer, fill in the joints using a mortar bag and tuck-pointing mortar. Take extra care to avoid smearing the mortar. You can tint the tuck-pointing mortar to complement the veneer.

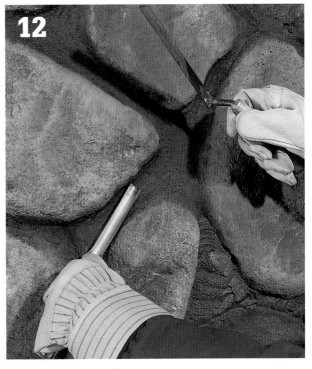

12

Smooth the joints with a jointing tool once the mortar is firm. Once the mortar is dry to the touch, use a dry whisk broom to remove loose mortar—water or chemicals can leave permanent stains.

Mortarless Brick Veneer

An interesting new siding product is now available that mimics the appearance and durability of classic brick but installs as easily as any other siding material. Mortarless brick veneer systems use stackable bricks to create an appealing façade on wood, steel, or concrete structures. The high-strength concrete bricks are long-lasting—manufacturers offer warranties up to 50 years. And because brick veneer does not require mortar, installation is well within the capabilities of interested homeowners.

Veneer bricks are available in 3-inch and 4-inch heights and are either 8 inches or 9 inches long, depending on the producer. Bricks weigh approximately 5 pounds each and add 3¼ inches to the face of walls. While veneer brick systems can be used in both new construction and remodel projects, application is restricted due to the added load: up to 30 feet high on standard wood-framed walls. Consult with a professional builder or structural engineer for walls taller than 30 feet, as well as sections of wall above roofs.

Prior to installation, make sure the framing and wall substrate is sound and the house adequately insulated. Extend all plumbing and electrical pipes, boxes, and meters to accommodate the additional thickness created by the veneer brick and furring strips.

The following pages discuss the installation of brick veneer siding on standard wood-framed walls. All openings require extra support in the form of ¾-inch plywood lintels. Lintel size is determined by the width of the opening and the brick installation method over the opening (soldier coursing shown here). Contact the manufacturer or product producer for information regarding lintel sizing, as well as installation of veneer brick on other framing styles.

Tools & Materials ▸

Tape measure	¾" plywood
Chalk line	Furring strips
4-ft. level	Flashing
Utility knife	Self-adhesive
Circular saw	waterproof
Miter saw	membrane (1 × 3,
with diamond	1 × 4, 1 × 6)
masonry-cutting	Scrap 2 × 4
blade or wet	Corrosion-resistant
masonry saw	wood screws
Hammer drill with	(#10 × 2½",
masonry bits	#10 × 4")
Cordless drill with	Outside corner strips
various drivers	Starter strips
Rubber mallet	Veneer bricks
Caulk gun	Outside corner blocks
Work gloves	Inside corner blocks
Safety glasses	Windowsill block
Dust mask	Construction adhesive
Earplugs	Exterior-grade caulk

Brick veneer siding attaches to your house with mechanical fasteners, so you can achieve the appeal of brick without the mess of mortar.

Tips for Installing Brick Veneer Siding

Brick veneer is stacked in courses with staggered joints, much like traditional brick. However, the first course of the mortarless system is installed on a starter strip and fastened with corrosion-resistant screws to 1 × 3 furring strips at each stud location. Bricks are then fastened every fourth course thereafter. At outside corners, a specialty strip is fastened to 1 × 4 furring strips. Corner blocks for both outside and inside corners are secured with screws and construction adhesive.

Before installing brick veneer siding, make sure all openings are properly sealed. For best results, use a self-adhesive waterproof membrane. Install the bottom strip first, then the side strips so they overlap the bottom strip. Place the top strip to overlap the sides. Install drip edge flashing where appropriate.

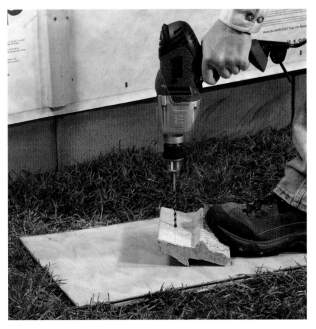

Cut veneer brick using a miter saw with a diamond blade or a wet masonry saw. When cutting brick, protect yourself with heavy work gloves, safety glasses, earplugs, and a dust mask. See pages 160 to 161 for more brick-cutting tips.

Predrill holes in bricks that require fastening using a hammer drill with a ³⁄₁₆" masonry bit. Position the brick face-up on the ground and secure with your foot. Drill through the notch in the top portion of the brick, holding the drill bit at 90° to the ground.

How to Install Mortarless Brick Veneer Siding

Snap a level chalk line ¾" above the foundation on each wall of the house. Align the bottom end of furring strips above the chalk line. Fasten 1 × 3 furring strips at each stud location with #10 × 2½" corrosion-resistant wood screws. Install 1 × 4 furring strips at outside corners and 1 × 6s at inside corners.

For each opening, cut ¾" plywood lintels to a size of 15" high × 12" longer than the width of the opening. Center the lintel above the opening so 6" extends beyond each side of the frame, and fasten to framing with #10 screws. Install an aluminum drip edge above the window frame, then wrap the lintel and flashing with a strip of self-adhesive waterproof membrane.

At outside corners, position the first section of corner strip 2" above the chalk line. Plumb the strip using a 4-ft. level, then fasten to the framing with #10 × 4" screws every 10" on alternate sides.

Position the starter strip at the chalk line with the flange beneath the ends of the furring strips. Do not overlap corner strips. At inside corners, cut back the starter strip to so it falls 3½" short of adjacent walls. Level the strip, then secure to the framing with #10 × 4" corrosion-resistant wood screws at each furring location.

At the notch in each corner block, predrill a hole at a 30° angle using a hammer drill and a ³⁄₁₆" masonry bit. Place a veneer brick on the starter strip for reference, then slide the first corner block down the corner strip and position it so the bottom edge falls ½" below the bottom edge of the brick. Fasten the brick to the strip with #10 × 2½" wood screws.

Continue to install corner blocks using #10 × 2½" screws and construction adhesive between courses. For the top of the corner, measure the remaining length and cut a piece of corner strip to size. Fasten blocks to this loose length, cutting the final piece to size if necessary (see page 167). Secure one last block to the existing corner using construction adhesive, then fit the new assembly in place and fasten with #10 × 2½" screws.

For inside corners, predrill holes at 30° angles into inside corner blocks. As with outside corners, position the first block so the bottom edge is ½" below the bottom edge of the first course of veneer brick. Fasten the block to the framing with #10 × 4" wood screws. Continue installing blocks with #10 screws and construction adhesive between each course.

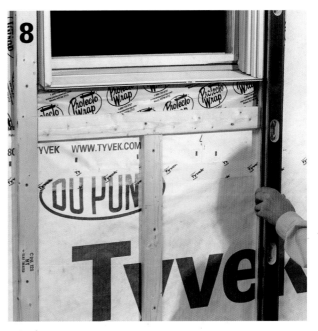

To create the best overall appearance, place a row of bricks on the starter strip so they extend past the width of the most prominent opening on each wall. Place a brick on the second course at each end of the opening, so each sits evenly above the joint of two bricks below. Sight down from the edges of the opening's frame and adjust the entire row to find a pattern that yields the least amount of small pieces of brick around the opening.

(continued)

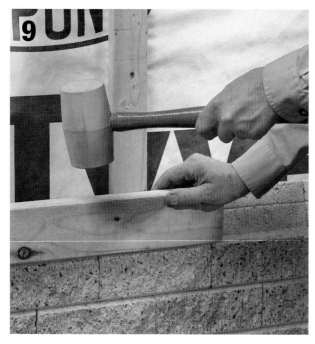

Predrill holes through veneer bricks for the first course (see page 167). Following the established pattern, install bricks on starter strip. At corners, cut bricks to size (see page 167) so they fit snugly against the blocks. Set bricks using a scrap 2 × 4 and rubber mallet to help maintain consistent course alignment.

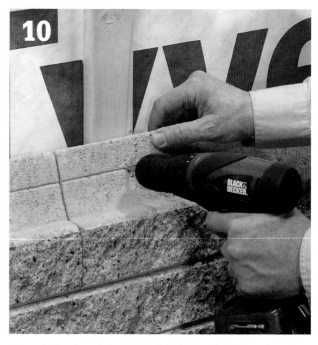

At each furring strip, hold bricks flat against the wall and secure to the framing with #10 × 2½" screws. Drive screws until the head touches the brick. Do not overtighten.

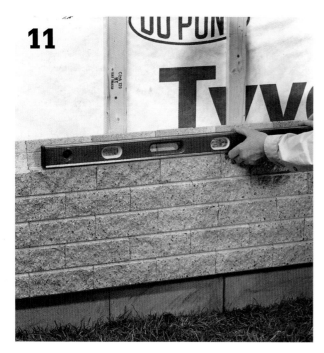

Fill the brick courses using bricks from different pallets to blend slight variance in color. Set bricks using a scrap of 2 × 4 and a rubber mallet. Check every fourth course for level before fastening bricks to the framing at each furring strip.

To install sill blocks below the widow, fasten a horizontal 1 × 3 furring strip under the window frame extending ⅛" longer than the cumulative width of the sill blocks. Install bricks up to the top of the furring strip, cutting to fit as needed, and fasten each with two #10 × 2½" wood screws. Apply construction adhesive along the top of the furring strip and bricks.

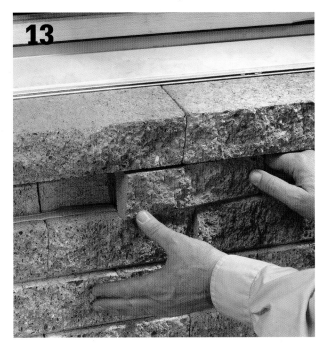

13

Install the sills, angling them downward slightly, and secure with #10 × 4" wood screws, toenailing through the ends or bottom of the sill into the framing. Cut brick filler pieces to bridge the gap between the sill and the last full course of brick; make sure the pieces align with the rest of the course. Install the pieces with construction adhesive. Seal the gap between the window frame and the sill with exterior-grade caulk.

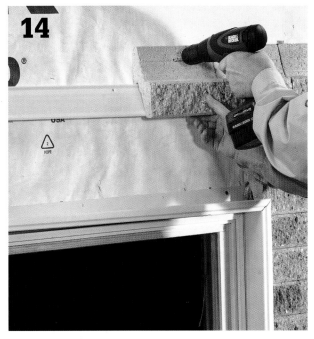

14

Continue installing brick along the openings to a height no more than the width of one brick. Cut a piece of starter strip to length, align it with the courses on either side of the opening, and secure to the framing with #10 × 2½" screws. Install a course of bricks on the starter strip, fastening them with #10 screws.

15

Cut bricks for the soldier course to length, then install vertically with two #10 × 2½" screws each. For the final brick, cut off the top portion and secure in place with construction adhesive. For a more symmetrical look, place cut bricks in the center of the course.

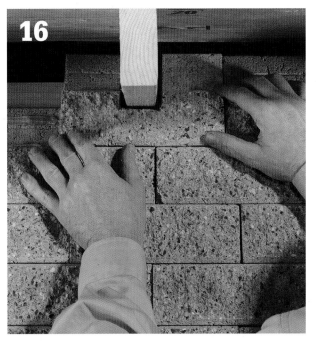

16

At the tops of walls, install 1 × 3 horizontal furring strips. Secure the second to the last course of bricks to the framing with #10 × 2½" screws, then install the last course with construction adhesive. Notch bricks to fit around joists or cut at an angle for gable walls.

Stucco

Prized for its weather resistance, durability, and timeless beauty, stucco has long been one of the most popular exterior wall finishes. As a building material, stucco is essentially an exterior plaster made of Portland cement, sand, and water. Other ingredients may include lime, masonry cement, and various special additives for enhancing properties like crack resistance, workability, and strength. With a few exceptions, stucco is applied much as it has been for centuries—a wet mix is troweled onto the wall in successive layers, with the final coat providing the finished color and any decorative surface texture desired.

The two traditional stucco systems are the three-coat system used for standard wood-framed walls, and the two-coat system used for masonry walls, like brick, poured concrete, and concrete block. And today, there's a third process—the one-coat system—which allows you to finish standard framed walls with a single layer of stucco, saving you money and considerable time and labor over traditional three-coat applications. Each of these systems is described in detail on the next page.

The following pages show you an overview of the materials and basic techniques for finishing a wall with stucco. While cladding an entire house or addition is a job for professional masons, smaller projects and repair work can be much more doable for the less experienced. Fortunately, all the stucco materials you need are available in premixed form, so you can be sure of getting the right blend of ingredients for each application (see page 174). During your planning, consult with the local building department to learn about requirements for surface preparation, fire ratings for walls, control joints, and other critical factors.

Tools & Materials ▸

Aviation snips	Grade D
Stapler	building paper
Hammer	Heavy-duty staples
Level	1½" galvanized
Cement mixer	roofing nails
Wheelbarrow	Self-furring
Mortar hawk	galvanized metal
Square-end trowel	lath (min. 2.5 lb.)
Raking tool	Metal stucco edging
Darby	Flashing
or screed board	Stucco mix
Wood float	(see page 174)
Texturing tools	Nonsag polyurethane
	sealant

Stucco is one of the most durable and low-maintenance wall finishes available, but it requires getting each stage of the installation right, as well as the mix of the stucco itself. For this reason, DIYers may want to limit their stucco work to small structures or to repair work only.

Stucco Systems ▸

Three-coat stucco is the traditional application for stud-framed walls covered with plywood, oriented strand board (OSB), or rigid foam insulation sheathing. It starts with two layers of Grade D building paper for a moisture barrier. The wall is then covered with self-furring, expanded metal lath fastened to the framing with galvanized nails.

The first layer of stucco, called the scratch coat, is pressed into the lath, then smoothed to a flat layer about ⅜" thick. While still wet, the stucco is "scratched" with a raking tool to create keys or "tooth" for the next layer to adhere to.

The brown coat is the next layer. It's about ⅜" thick and brings the wall surface to within ⅛ to ¼" of the finished thickness. Imperfections here can easily telegraph through the thin final coat, so the surface must be smooth and flat. To provide tooth for the final layer, the brown coat is finished with a wood float for a slightly roughened texture.

The finish coat completes the treatment, bringing the surface flush with the stucco trim pieces and providing the color and decorative texture, if desired. There are many options for texturing stucco; a few of the classic ones are shown on page 176.

Two-coat stucco is the standard treatment for masonry walls. This system is the same as a three-coat treatment but without a scratch coat. The base coat on a 2-coat system is the same as the brown coat on a three-coat system. For the base coat to bond well, the masonry surface must be clean, unpainted, and sufficiently porous. You can test this by spraying water onto the surface: if the water beads and runs down the wall, you should apply bonding adhesive before applying the base coat or you can fasten self-furring metal lath directly to the wall, then apply a full three-coat stucco treatment.

One-coat stucco is a single-layer system for finishing framed walls prepared with a waterproof barrier and metal lath (as with a three-coat system). This treatment calls for one-coat, fiberglass-reinforced stucco, a special formulation that contains 12" alkali-resistant fiberglass fiber, and other additives to combine high-performance characteristics with greatly simplified application. This stucco is applied in a ⅜ - to ⅝"-thick layer using standard techniques. QUIKRETE One Coat Fiberglass Reinforced Stucco meets code requirements for a one hour firewall over wood and form systems.

Premixed Stucco Products ▶

Finding the right blend of ingredients and mixing to the proper consistency are critical to the success of any stucco project. Premixed stucco eliminates the guesswork by giving you the perfect blend in each bag, along with mixing and curing instructions for a professional-quality job. All of the stucco products shown here are sold in complete form, meaning all you do is add water before application. Be sure to follow the mixing and curing instructions carefully for each product.

Scratch & Brown, Base Coat stucco: Use this premixed stucco for both the scratch and brown coats of a three-coat application or for the base coat of a two-coat system. You can apply the mixed stucco with a trowel or an approved sprayer. Available in 80 lb. bags in gray color. Each bag yields approximately 0.83 cu. ft. or an applied coverage of approximately 27 sq. ft. at ⅜" thickness.

Finish Coat stucco: Use this stucco for the finish coat on both three-coat and two-coat systems. You can also use it to create a decorative textured finish over one-coat stucco. Apply Finish Coat stucco to a minimum thickness of ⅛", then texture the surface as desired. Available in gray and white for achieving a full range of colors (see below). Coverage of 80-lb. bag is approximately 70 sq. ft. at ⅛" thickness.

One Coat Fiberglass Reinforced Stucco: Complete your stucco application in one step with this convenient all-in-one stucco mix. It's available in gray and white for creating a wide range of colors (see below). You can texture the surface of the single layer or add a top coat of Finish Coat stucco for special decorative effects. Available in 80-lb. bags. An 80-lb. bag covers approximately 25 sq. ft. of wall at ⅜" thickness.

Stucco & Mortar Color: Available in 20 standard colors, Stucco & Mortar Color is a permanent liquid colorant that you blend with the stucco mix before application. Some colors are for use with gray stucco mix, while many others are compatible with white mix. For best results, combine the liquid colorant with the mixing water before adding the dry stucco mix, then blend thoroughly until the color is uniform.

How to Prepare Framed Walls for Stucco

1

Attach building paper over exterior wall sheathing using heavy-duty staples or roofing nails. Overlap sheets by 4". Often, two layers of paper are required or recommended; consult your local building department for code requirements in your area.

2

Install self-furring expanded metal lath over the building paper with 1½" galvanized roofing nails (don't use aluminum nails) driven into the wall studs every 6". Overlap sheets of lath by 1" on horizontal seams and 2" on vertical seams. Install the lath with the rougher side facing out.

3

Install metal edging for clean, finished lines at vertical edges of walls. Install casing bead along the top of stuccoed areas and weep screed (or drip screed) along the bottom edges, as applicable. Make sure all edging is level and plumb, and fasten it with galvanized roofing nails. Add flashing as needed over windows and doors.

4

Use aviation snips to trim sheets of lath or cut edging materials to length. Cut lath and edging can be very sharp, so always wear gloves when working with these materials.

How to Finish Walls with Stucco

For a three-coat system, mix the stucco to a trowel-able consistency and apply it with a square trowel, working from the bottom up. Press the stucco into the lath, then screed and smooth the surface for a uniform thickness. When the coat hardens enough to hold a finger impression, scratch ⅛"-deep horizontal grooves into the surface with a raking tool.

After moist-curing the scratch coat for 48 hours, mix stucco for the brown coat (or base coat for two-coat system) and apply it in a 3/8"-thick layer. Use a straight board or a darby to screed the surface so it's flat and even. When the stucco has lost its sheen, float it with a wood trowel to roughen the surface. Moist-cure the coat for 48 hours as directed.

Variation: For a one-coat application, mix the stucco and apply it in a ⅜"-thick layer, working from the bottom up and forcing it in to completely embed the lath. Screed the surface flat with a darby or board. When the surface loses its sheen, finish-trowel or texture the surface as desired. Cure the coat as directed. Seal all joints around building elements with polyurethane sealant.

Mix the finish coat and apply it in a ⅛"-thick (minimum) layer, working from the bottom up. Complete large sections or entire walls at one time for color consistency. Texture the surface as desired. Cure the coat as directed. Seal all joints around building elements with polyurethane sealant.

How to Finish Stucco

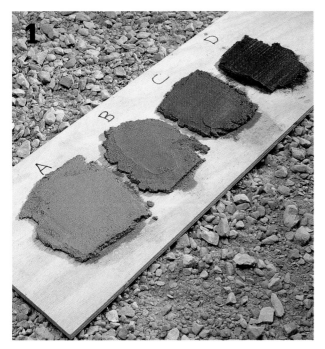

Test the coloring of finish stucco by adding different proportions of colorant and mix. Let the samples dry to see their true finished color. For the application batches, be sure to use the same proportions when mixing each batch.

Mix the finish batch so it contains slightly more water than the scratch and brown coats. The mix should still stay on the mortar hawk without running.

Finish Option: Cover a float with carpet to make an ideal tool for achieving a float-finish texture. Experiment on a small area.

Finish Option: Achieve a wet-dash finish by flinging, or dashing, stucco onto the surface. Let the stucco cure undisturbed.

Finish Option: For a dash-trowel texture, dash the surface with stucco using a whisk broom (left), then flatten the stucco by troweling over it.

Surface-bonding Cement

Surface bonding cement is a stucco-like compound that you can use to dress up your concrete and cinder block walls. It also adds strength, durability, and water resistance to the walls.

What distinguishes surface bonding cement from stucco is the addition of fiberglass to the blend of Portland cement and sand. The dry mixture is combined with water and acrylic fortifier to form a cement plaster that can bond with concrete, brick, or block for an attractive, water-resistant coating.

Before applying the bonding cement, make sure you have a very clean surface with no crumbling masonry, so the coating can form a durable bond. Because surface bonding cement dries quickly, it's important to mist the brick or block with water before applying the cement so the cement dries slowly. As with most masonry projects, the need to dampen the wall increases in very dry weather.

The bonding cement can be used on both mortared and mortarless walls, and on both load-bearing and non-load-bearing walls. However, it is not recommended for walls higher than 15 courses of block.

Tools & Materials ▸

Garden hose with spray attachment
Bucket
Wheelbarrow
Mortar hawk
Square-end trowel
Groover
Caulk gun
Surface bonding cement
Concrete acrylic fortifier
Tint (optional)
Silicone caulk

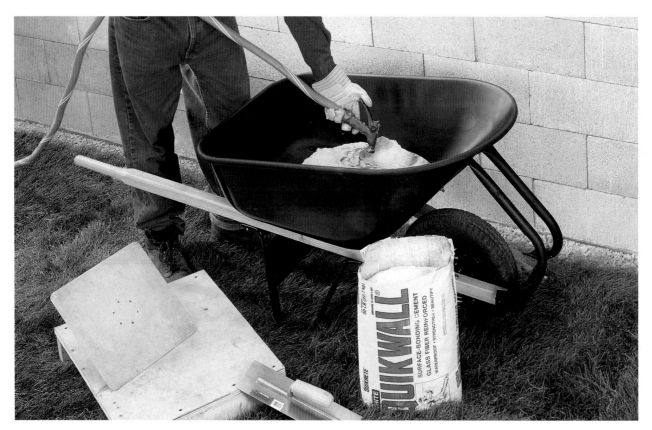

Mix small batches of dry surface bonding cement, water, and concrete acrylic fortifier according to the manufacturer's instructions until you get a feel for how much coating you can apply before it hardens. An accelerant in the cement causes the mix to harden quickly—within 30 to 90 minutes, depending on weather conditions. The cement can be tinted before application.

How to Finish Walls with Surface Bonding Cement

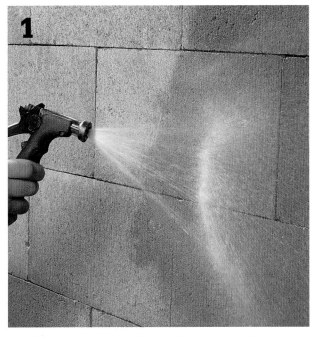

1

Starting near the top of the wall, mist a 2 × 5-ft. section on one side of the wall with water to prevent the blocks from absorbing moisture from the cement once the coating is applied.

2

Mix the cement in small batches according to the manufacturer's instructions, and apply a 1/16-to 1/8"-thick layer to the damp blocks using a square-end trowel. Spread the cement evenly by angling the trowel slightly and making broad upward strokes.

3

Use a wet trowel to smooth the surface and create the texture of your choice. Rinse the trowel frequently to keep it clean and wet.

4

To prevent random cracking, use a groover to cut control joints from the top to the bottom of the wall every 4 ft. for a 2-ft.-high wall, and every 8 ft. for a 4-ft.-high wall. Seal hardened joints with silicone caulk.

Installing Exterior Trim Details

Siding or roofing projects usually involve installing other ventilation, drainage, or trim details. A reroof is the perfect time to add more heat vents to improve your attic ventilation. New siding looks tidier if you follow it with fresh aluminum fascia coverings that complement the siding color. Before you embark on that new siding, consider framing your eaves with soffits. Or, maybe it's time to switch to seamless gutters, finish those cornices and gables with wood trim, or add some decorative shutters. These sorts of trim and detailing projects are the focus of this chapter. They may seem like a bit of a departure from other sections of this book, but these details will give your major roofing or siding project the finishing touch it deserves.

In this chapter:

- Soffits & Vents
- Aluminum Soffits
- Aluminum Fascia
- Wood Soffits
- New Vents
- Vinyl Gutters
- Seamless Gutters
- Wrapping Posts & Beams
- Finishing Cornice & Gable
- Brickmold
- Decorative Trim
- Custom Shutters

Soffits & Vents

An effective ventilation system equalizes temperatures on both sides of the roof, which helps keep your house cooler in the summer and prevents ice dams along the roof eaves in cold climates.

One strategy for increasing roof ventilation is to add more of the existing types of vents. Or, if you're reroofing, consider replacing all of your roof vents with a continuous ridge vent (pages 86 to 87). You can increase intake ventilation by adding more soffit vents. If you're replacing your soffits with aluminum soffits, install vented soffit panels that allow air intake (pages 184 to 186).

Determining Ventilation Requirements

Measure attic floor space to determine how much ventilation you need. You should have 1 sq. ft. each of intake and outtake ventilation for every 300 sq. ft. of unheated attic floor space.

Roof vent (outtake)

Insulation baffle

Roof sheathing

Fascia

Unheated attic space

Vapor barrier

Attic insulation blanket (between ceiling joists)

Rafter

Soffit panel

Heated room space

Soffit vent (intake)

Air flow

Shown cutaway for clarity

Sufficient airflow prevents heat buildup in your attic, and it helps protect your roof from damage caused by condensation or ice. A typical ventilation system has vents in the soffits to admit fresh air, which flows upward beneath the roof sheathing and exits through the roof vents.

Types of Vents

Soffit vents can be added to increase airflow into attics on houses with a closed soffit system.

Continuous soffit vents provide even airflow into attics. They are usually installed during new construction, but they can be added as retrofits to unvented soffit panels.

Roof vents can be added near the ridge line when you need to increase outtake ventilation. Fixed roof vents are easy to install and have no mechanical parts that can break down.

Vented soffit panels are used with aluminum soffits to allow airflow along the eaves.

Gable and dormer vents generally are installed to increase ventilation. The vents come in a variety of styles and colors to match the siding.

Continuous ridge vents create an even outtake airflow because they span the entire ridge. Barely noticeable from the ground, ridge vents can be added at any time.

Aluminum Soffits

Older soffits may be weathered or rotted and may not allow adequate airflow. If more than 15 percent of your soffits need to be repaired, your best option is to replace them. This project shows how to completely remove the old soffits and fascia, and install aluminum soffits, which are maintenance free. If your old subfascia is in good condition, it will not need to be replaced.

The project starting on the opposite page details the installation of soffits on an eaves system that has rafter lookouts. The soffits are installed directly beneath these lookouts. If your eaves do not have rafter lookouts, follow the instructions starting on page 186. This project also shows how to install soffits around corners.

For both eaves systems, an F-channel serves as a mounting channel to hold the soffits in place along the house. You can also install the channel along the subfascia, as shown in step 4 on page 185, or you can nail the soffits directly to the subfascia, as shown in step 4 on page 187. Drive nail heads flush with the surface. Driving the nails too deep can knock the soffits out of shape and prevent movement. Since the soffits will receive addition nailing when the fascia is installed, you don't need to drive a nail in every V-groove in the soffits.

To cut soffits, use a circular saw with a fine-tooth blade installed backward. Don't cut all of your panels at the start of the job since the width will probably change slightly as you move across the house.

Use vented soffit panels to work in conjunction with roof or attic vents. This improves airflow underneath the roof, which prevents moisture damage and ice dams. Provide 1 square foot of soffit vents for every 150 sqare feet of unheated attic space. For a consistent appearance, make sure all of the fins on the soffit vents are pointed in the same direction.

Tools & Materials ▸

Flat pry bar	F-channel
Hammer	(mounting channel)
Circular saw with	1¼" aluminum
fine-tooth metal	trim nails
blade (installed	16d common nails
backward)	Nailing strips
Drill	Drip edge
Tape measure	2¼" deck screws
Aviation snips	8d box nails
Level	Subfascia, if needed
Framing square	(2 × 4, 1 × 8,
Soffit panels	or 2 × 8)
T-channel	

Labels on image: Support ledge for soffit panels — Cornice cover removed — Fascia cover — Soffit panel — Support channel for soffit panels

Install a new soffit system if your old system has failed, or if pests have infested the open eaves areas of your roof overhang. A complete soffit system consists of fabricated fascia covers, soffit panels (nonventilated or ventilated), and support channels that hold the panels at the sides of your house. Most soffit systems sold at building centers are made of aluminum.

How to Install Aluminum Soffits (with Rafter Lookouts)

Remove trim, soffits, and fascia along the eaves using a flat pry bar. If the eaves contain debris, such as bird nests or rotted wood, clean them out.

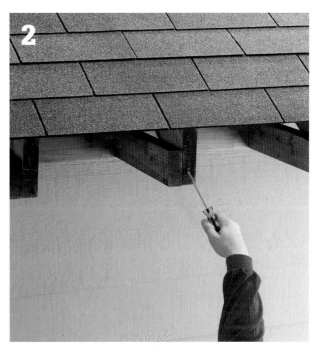

Check the rafters and rafter lookouts for decay or damage. Repair or replace them as needed.

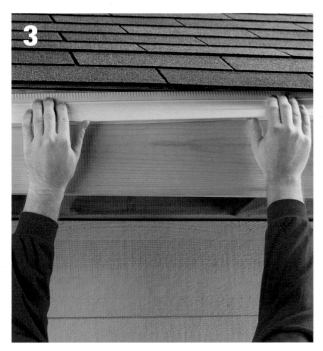

Install new 1 × 8 or 2 × 8 subfascia over the rafters and rafter lookouts using 16d nails. Butt subfascia boards together at rafter or rafter lookout locations. Install drip edge at the top of the subfascia. Leave a ¹⁄₁₆" gap between the drip edge and the subfascia for the fascia to fit.

Install F-channels for the soffit panels along the bottom inside edge of the subfascia and along the outside wall of the house directly below the rafter lookouts. If more than one piece of channel is needed, butt pieces together.

(continued)

<table>
<tr>
<td></td>
<td></td>
<td></td>
</tr>
<tr>
<td>

If the soffit panels will span more than 16", or if your house is subjected to high winds, add nailing strips to provide additional support.

</td>
<td>

Measure the distance between the mounting channels, subtract ⅛", and cut soffits to size. Slide the soffit panels in place, fitting the ends inside the mounting channels. Nail the panels to the nailing strips, if you've installed them.

</td>
<td>

Install soffit panels in the remaining spaces, cutting them to fit as needed. When finished, install the fascia (pages 188 to 189).

</td>
</tr>
</table>

How to Install Aluminum Soffits (without Rafter Lookouts)

<table>
<tr>
<td></td>
<td></td>
</tr>
<tr>
<td>

Remove the old soffits and fascia, following step 1 on page 185. Place a level at the bottom of the subfascia board level across to the house, and make a mark. Measure down from the mark a distance equal to the thickness of the soffits (usually about ¼"). Do this on each end of the wall. Snap a chalk line between the lower marks.

</td>
<td>

Start the F-channel at a corner and align the bottom edge with the chalk line. Nail the channel to the wall at stud locations using 8d box nails. If more than one F-channel is needed, butt the pieces together.

</td>
</tr>
</table>

3

At corners, cut a 2 × 4 to fit between the house and the inside corner of the subfascia to provide support for the T-channel. Notch the 2 × 4 as needed, then nail in place so when the T-channel is installed, it will be aligned with the F-channel. Cut the T-channel to fit. Place it against the 2 × 4, setting the back edge inside the F-channel, and nail in place.

4

Measure between the F-channel and the outside edge of the subfascia. Subtract ¼" and cut the soffits to size. For corners, miter the panels to fit the T-channel. Install the first panel inside the channel. Make sure the panel is square to the subfascia using a framing square. Nail the panel to the subfascia at the V-grooves. Slide the next panel against the first, locking them together. Nail the panel in place. Install remaining panels the same way.

Variations for Installing Aluminum Soffits

Straight corners are made by installing the T-channel parallel with one of the F-channels. Align the outside edge of the T-channel with the outside edge of the installed F-channel. Keep the T-channel back ¼" from the outside of the subfascia, and nail it in place. Install the soffits in the channels.

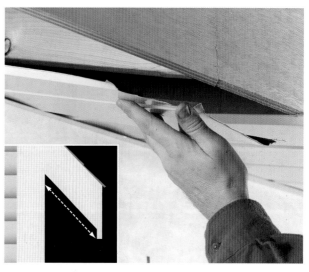

Inclined overhangs allow soffits to run the same angle as the rafters. At the end of the rafter overhangs, measure from the bottom of the rafter to the bottom of the subfascia. Add the thickness of the soffits, then measure down from the rafters along the wall and make a mark at this distance. Do this on each end of the wall. Snap a chalk line between the marks. Align the bottom of the F-channel with the chalk line, nail the channel to the wall, then install the soffits.

Aluminum Fascia

Fascia fits under the drip edge and against the subfascia to provide a smooth transition from the roof to the eaves. You may need to temporarily remove any nails in the face of the drip edge so the fascia can slide in behind it. If your roof does not have drip edge, install a finish trim, such as undersill, at the top of the subfascia to receive the fascia.

If you're also replacing your gutters, take down the gutters first, then install the fascia. If you don't want to remove the gutters, you can slip the fascia behind them while they're in place.

Fascia is nailed along the lip covering the soffits, and the top is held in place by the drip edge, so it doesn't require any face nailing.

The fascia is installed over the subfascia to cover the exposed edges of the soffits and enhance the appearance of your home. The fascia is usually the same color and material as your soffits.

Tools & Materials ▸

Hammer	Chalk line
Aviation snips	Fascia
Tape measure	Aluminum trim nails

How to Install Aluminum Fascia

1

Remove the old fascia, if necessary. Measure from the top of the drip edge to the bottom of the soffits, and subtract ¼". Cut the fascia to this measurement by snapping a chalk line across the face and cutting with aviation snips. (This cut edge will be covered by the drip edge.) *Tip: If your old fascia is wood and still in good shape, you can install aluminum fascia over it without removing it.*

2

Slide the cut edge of the fascia behind the drip edge. Place the bottom lip over the soffits. Make sure the fascia is tight against the soffits and against the subfascia, then nail through the lip into the subfascia. Nail approximately every 16" at a V-groove location in the soffits.

To overlap fascia panels, cut the ridge on the lip of the first panel 1" from the end using aviation snips. Place the second panel over the first, overlapping the seam by 1". Nail the fascia in place.

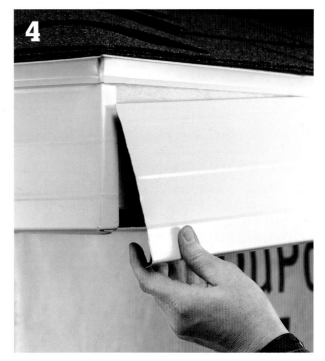

At outside corners, cut the lip and top edge of the first panel 1" from the end. Place a piece of wood 1" from the end, and bend the panel to form a 90° angle. Install the panel at the corner. Cut a 45° angle in the lip of the second panel. Align the end of this panel with the corner, overlapping the first panel.

For inside corners, cut and bend the first panel back 1" from the end to make a tab. Install the panel. On the second panel, cut a 45° angle in the lip. Slide the panel over the first panel, butting the end against the adjacent fascia. Nail the panel in place.

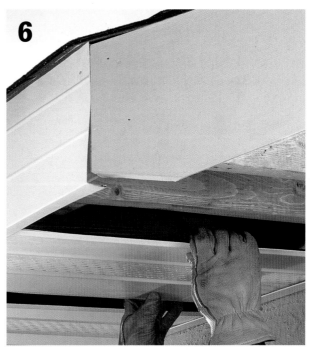

Install soffit panels to close off the area between the fascia cover and the exterior wall (see pages 184 to 185).

Wood Soffits

Wood soffits are typically used on houses with wood or fiber-cement siding, and are painted the same color as the trim. To see how the soffits fit in relation to the fascia and rafters, refer to the photo on page 256. You can use plywood or engineered wood for the soffits. Engineered wood has the advantage of being treated to resist termites and fungus, and it's more resistant to warping and shrinking. Plywood has the advantage of being less expensive. If your soffits are more than 24" wide, install a nailing strip between panels to hold the seams tightly together.

When replacing soffits, you may need to remove the top course of siding and any trim pieces under the old soffits before starting the new installation. Remove the pieces carefully, then reinstall them once the soffit job is finished.

Tools & Materials ▸

Hammer
Circular saw
Level
Chalk line
Caulk gun
Paintbrush
Drill
Jigsaw
⅜" plywood
16d box nails
6d corrosion-resistant
   nails

2 × 2 lumber
Acrylic latex caulk
Vents
Primer
Paint

Wood soffits cover the eaves area between the fascia and siding. Painted soffit moldings beneath the soffits give the house a finished look. Soffit vents installed at regular intervals play a vital role in the home's ventilation system.

How to Install Wood Soffits

Hold a level against the bottom edge of the subfascia and level across to make a mark on the wall. Do this on both ends of the wall, then snap a chalk line between the marks.

Align the bottom edge of 2 × 2 lumber with the chalk line. Nail the lumber to wall studs using 16d nails.

Measure the distance from the wall to the outside of the subfascia, subtract ¼", and rip the soffits to this width. Apply primer to the soffits. If using wood that's already primed, apply primer to the cut edges only.

Place the soffit against the 2 × 2 and subfascia, staying ⅛" from the edges. Nail in place using 6d nails. Install remaining soffits, keeping a ⅛" gap between panels. Caulk the gaps between soffits and between the soffits and wall. Paint soffits as desired. Let the paint dry.

Mark the vent locations in the soffits by holding the vent in place and tracing around it. Drill starter holes at opposite corners of the outline, then cut out the opening with a jigsaw. Install the vent using the fasteners that came with it. Do this at each vent location.

Variation: If the soffits have rafter lookouts, you don't need to install 2 × 2s. Instead, nail the soffits directly to the rafter headers and lookouts. Make sure soffit seams fall midway across rafter lookouts.

New Vents

If you need more ventilation for your attic, but you don't want to replace your soffits or embark on a roofing project, you can add vents to your existing wood soffits and roof.

This project shows how to add soffit vents for air intake, and how to add roof vents for air outtake. These additional vents increase the airflow under your roof, helping to eliminate heat buildup in your attic.

Tools & Materials ▸

Hammer
Pry bar
Chalk line
Caulk gun
Tape measure
Drill
Jigsaw
Utility knife
Rubber gasket nails

Roof cement
Stainless steel
  screws
Soffit vent covers
Roof vents
Siliconized
  acrylic caulk
Screwdriver

How to Install Soffit Vents

Examine the eaves area from inside your attic to make sure there is nothing obstructing airflow from the soffits. If insulation is blocking the air passage, install insulation baffles.

Draw a cutout for the soffit vent cover on the soffit panel. Center the vents between the fascia and the side of the house. The cover outline should be ¼" smaller on all sides than the soffit vent cover.

Drill a starter hole, then cut the vent openings with a jigsaw.

Caulk the flanges of the vent cover. Screw the vent cover to the soffit. *Tip: For visual effect, install new vent covers with the louvers pointing in the same direction.*

How to Install Roof Vents

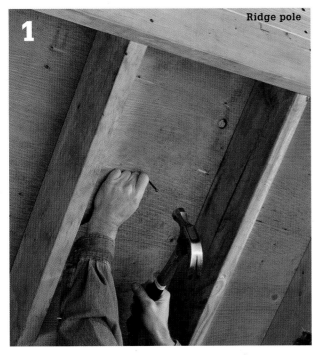

Ridge pole

Mark the location for the roof vent by driving a nail through the roof sheathing. Center the nail between rafters 16" to 24" from the ridge pole.

Center a vent cover over the nail on the outside of the roof. Outline the base flange of the vent cover on the shingles, then remove shingles in an area 2" inside the outline. Mark the roof vent hole using the marker nail as a centerpoint. Cut the hole using a reciprocating saw or jigsaw.

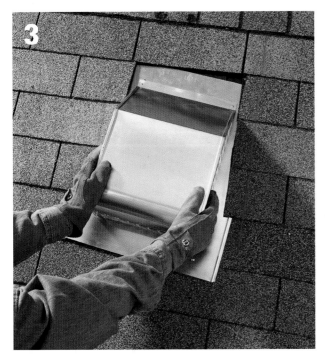

Apply roof cement to the underside of the base flange. Set the vent cover in position, slipping the flange under the shingles, centered over the vent-hole cutout.

Secure the roof vent to the sheathing with rubber gasket nails on all sides of the flange. Tack down any loose shingles. Do not nail through the flange when attaching shingles.

Vinyl Gutters

Installing a snap-together vinyl gutter system is a manageable task for most do-it-yourselfers. Snap-together gutter systems are designed for ease of installation, requiring no fasteners other than the screws used to attach the gutter hangers to the fascia.

Before you purchase new gutters, create a detailed plan and cost estimate. Include all of the necessary parts, not just the gutter and drain pipe sections—they make up only part of the total system. Test-fit the pieces on the ground before you begin the actual installation.

Vinyl snap-together gutter systems are easy to install and relatively inexpensive, and they won't rot or deteriorate. The slip joints allow for expansion and contraction, which contribute to their reliability and longevity.

Estimating Gutter Parts
- Gutter sections: Measure total length of run; add 15% for waste. Sold in 10-ft. lengths.
- Gutter hangers: One for every 2 ft. of gutter.
- Inside/outside corners: One per corner with no outlet.
- Connectors: Two per corner; one per 10 ft. of gutter.
- End caps (right or left): One per end.
- Downspout outlets: One for every 35 ft. of gutter.
- Downspout elbows: Three per downspout.
- Drainpipe: One pipe per downspout outlet. Measure gutter height and add 5 ft. for each pipe (for splash block outlet and waste). Sold in 10-ft. lengths.
- Drainpipe hangers: Two per drainpipe.

How to Install Vinyl Gutters

Mark a point at the high end of each gutter run, 1" from the top of the fascia. Snap chalk lines that slope ¼" per 10 ft. toward downspouts. For runs longer than 35 ft., mark a slope from a high point in the center toward downspouts at each end.

Install downspout outlets near the ends of gutter runs (at least one outlet for every 35 ft. of run). The tops of the outlets should be flush with the slope line, and they should align with end caps on the corners of the house.

Following the slope line, attach hangers or support clips for hangers for a complete run. Attach them to the fascia at 24" intervals using deck screws.

Following the slope line, attach outside and inside corners at all corner locations that don't have end caps.

Use a hacksaw to cut gutter sections to fit between outlets and corners. Attach the end caps and connect the gutter sections to the outlets. Cut and test-fit gutter sections to fit between outlets, allowing for expansion gaps.

Working on the ground, join the gutter sections together using connectors. Attach gutter hangers to the gutter (for models with support clips mounted on the fascia). Hang the gutters, connecting them to the outlets.

Cut a section of drainpipe to fit between two downspout elbows. One elbow should fit over the tail of the downspout outlet and the other should fit against the wall. Assemble the parts, slip the top elbow onto the outlet, and secure the other to the siding with a drainpipe hanger.

Cut a piece of drainpipe to fit between the elbow at the top of the wall and the end of the drainpipe run, staying at least 12" above the ground. Attach an elbow, and secure the pipe to the wall with a drainpipe hanger. Add accessories, such as splash blocks, to help channel water away from the house (inset).

Seamless Gutters

Seamless gutters are continuous lengths of gutters, rather than two or more sections fastened together. By eliminating the seams, you eliminate the potential for leaks. However, "seamless" is a bit of a misnomer. There are still seams at the corners and ends, which need to be sealed.

The gutters should extend slightly past the edge of the fascia, aligning with the edges of the roofing. The back edge of the gutter slides behind the drip edge. When preparing the gutters, zip screws are preferred over rivets. They don't require predrilling, and they can be unscrewed later.

Seamless gutters are fabricated on-site, or they can be delivered to your home at the specified length.

Tools & Materials ▸

Tape measure
Drill with ¼"
    hex-drive bit
Caulk gun
Chalk line
Hammer
Tin snips
Hacksaw
Gutters
Zip screws

Gutter sealant or
    silicone caulk
Hangers
Gutter outlets
Downspouts
End caps
Elbows
Hangers
Downspout brackets
End box

How to Install Seamless Gutters

At the fascia's midpoint, measure down from the drip edge and make a mark for the bottom of the gutter. Mark both ends of the fascia, adding a ¼" slope for every 10 ft. of gutter. Snap chalk lines between the marks.

Mark the downspout locations on the gutter. Set a gutter outlet at each mark, centered from front to back, and trace around it. Cut out the holes using aviation snips or a rotary saw.

Apply a bead of sealant under the lip of the outlet. Place the outlet in the hole in the gutter. Press firmly in place, then attach from the bottom side of the gutter using zip screws.

Place an end cap over the end of the gutter. Drive zip screws through the flange into the gutter. Apply ample sealant along the inside edges of the cap.

Apply a small bead of sealant on the bottom and sides inside a corner box. Slide the end of the gutter inside the box. Fasten the gutter and box together using zip screws. Apply ample sealant along the inside seam.

Clip gutter hangers to the gutter every 24". Lift the gutter into place, sliding the back side under the drip edge and aligning the bottom with the chalk line. Drive the nail or screw in each hanger through the fascia to install.

Fasten an elbow to the gutter outlet, driving a zip screw through each side. Hold another elbow in place against the house. Measure the distance between the elbows, adding 2" at each end for overlap. Cut a downspout to this length using a hacksaw. Crimp the corners of the downspout for easy insertion and fasten together. *Tip: Assemble the elbows and downspout so the top pieces always fit inside bottom pieces.*

Fasten downspout brackets to the wall for the top and bottom of the downspout and every 8 ft. in between. Cut a downspout that spans the length of the wall, and attach it to the elbow at the top. Install another elbow at the end of the downspout. Fasten the brackets to the downspout.

Wrapping Posts & Beams

Whether they support a porch roof or a deck, posts and beams can look spindly and plain. Rather than spend the money for large timbers, it is a common practice among builders to wrap the posts and beams with finish-grade lumber to give them a more proportional look. The finish-grade pine cladding shown here gives 4 × 4 posts and doubled 2 × 8 beams the look of more substantial stock.

Tools & Materials ▶

Basic hand tools
Finish lumber
Siding nails
Plywood strips

How to Wrap Posts & Beams

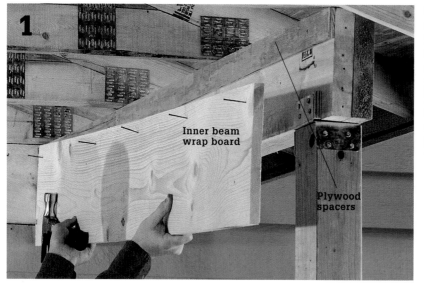

Cut cladding boards for the inner sides of the beams to the same length as the beams using finish lumber wide enough to cover the beams and any metal saddles or joiners. We used 1 × 10, but sanded ¾" plywood can be used instead. Attach the inner-side boards to the beams with 8d siding nails—in the project shown here, we added ½" plywood strips at the top and bottom of the beam to compensate for the ½" spacers in the metal post saddles.

Cut strips of wood to cover the bottoms of the beams. Position each strip next to a board cut the same size as the inner beam wrap. The difference in length between the side board and the bottom board should equal the distance of the beam overhang at the post. Preassemble the bottom board and side board by driving 8d finish nails at the butt joint, making sure to keep the joint square. Attach the assembly to the beam so the free end of the bottom board forms a butt joint with the inner beam wrap board.

Cut boards to create an end cap for each beam—we cut a piece of 1 × 10 to fit over the ends of the beam and the beam wrap, and attached it to a piece of 1 × 4 cut to cover the gap beneath the beam overhang. Nail end caps over the end of each beam.

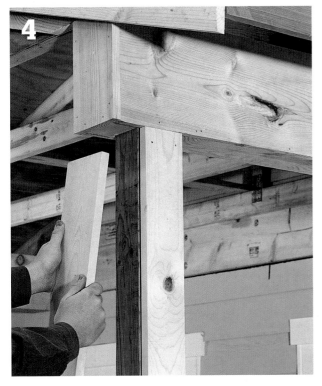

Cut boards for wrapping the posts so they span from the post bottoms to the beam bottoms. For a 4 × 4 post, two 1 × 4s and two 1 × 6s per post can be used. Nail a 1 × 6 to the front of the post overhanging ¾" on the outside edge. Nail a 1 × 4 to the outer face of the post butted against the 1 × 6.

Preassemble the other two wrap boards, nailing through the face of the 1 × 6 and into the edge of the 1 × 4. Set the assembly around the post, nailing the 1 × 6 to the post and nailing through the other 1 × 6 and into the edge of the 1 × 4 (there will be a slight gap between the second 1 × 4 and the post).

Cut pieces of finish lumber to fit around the bases of the posts (called post collars). We used 1 × 6 to create the bottom post collars and 1 × 4 to create the top collars, where the posts meet the beams. Nail the collars together with 4d finish nails. Cut pieces so the front collar board covers the end grain of the side boards. Cove molding around the tops of the collars gives a more finished look and sheds water.

Roof ledgers often are visible after the porch ceiling is installed, so cover the ledger with finish lumber. If the ledger protrudes past the siding, cut a furring strip to cover the gap between the inside face of the ledger cover and the siding. Cut the ledger cover and furring strips to fit, and install with 8d nails. If the ledger extends past the outer face of the beam, the easiest solution is to paint it to match the siding.

Furring strip

Cornices & Gables

The gable and the cornice are prominent features on many houses. The gable is the area just below the peak, which is usually covered with trim and siding material. The cornice, sometimes called the cornice return or the fascia return, is usually fitted with trim that squares off the corner where it meets the soffit. The project shown here involves putting the finishing touches on a new porch, but these areas commonly require repair as well.

Tools & Materials ▸

Basic hand tools
Miter box
Straightedge guide
Plywood
Framing lumber

Finish-grade lumber
Cove molding
Nails
Caulk

The cornice and gable are finished to match the siding and trim on your house. Use plywood or finish-grade lumber to make the cornice, and use siding that matches your house for the gable trim. Caulk seams at the peak of the gable, and between the fascia boards and the cornice (inset).

How to Install a Cornice

At each end of the front porch, measure the area from the end of the gable fascia to a spot about 6" inside the porch beam. Lay out a triangular piece of plywood or finish-grade lumber to fit the area using a carpenter's square to create right angles. Cut out the cornice pieces using a circular saw and straightedge.

Test-fit the cornice pieces over the ends of the porch gable, then install with 8d finish nails driven into the ends of the beams, and 4d nails driven up through the ends of the cornice pieces and into the underside of the gable fascia. Use a nail set to embed the heads of the nails below the surface of the wood, being careful not to split the cornice pieces.

How to Install Gable Trim

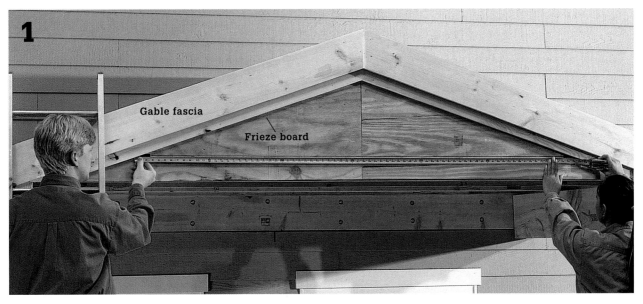

1

Gable fascia

Frieze board

Measure the dimensions of the area covered by the gable sheathing on the house. If you have installed fascia and frieze boards, measure from the bottom of the frieze boards. Add 2" of depth to the area to make sure that siding will cover the edge of the ceiling once the ceiling and soffits are installed. Snap a horizontal chalk line near the bottom of the gable sheathing to use as a reference line for installing the siding.

2

3

Mark a cutting line that matches the slope of the roof onto the end of one piece of siding. Use a framing square or a speed square to mark the slope line. *Option: Position a scrap board on the horizontal chalk line on the gable sheathing and mark the points where the edges of the board intersect with the frieze board. Connect the points to establish the slope line. Cut the siding or scrap board on the slope line and use it as a template to mark siding for cutting. Cut the bottom siding board to length.*

Use 4d siding nails to install the bottom siding board so it is flush with the bottom edges of the frieze boards—the bottom edge of the siding board should be 2" lower than the bottom of the gable sheathing. Cut the next siding board so it overlaps the first board from above, creating the same amount of exposed siding as in the rest of the house. Be careful to keep the siding level. Continue cutting and installing siding pieces until you reach the peak of the gable.

Brickmold

Brickmold is decorative trim that forms a transition between siding and windows or doors. It's usually made of pine or fir. Unless these moldings are maintained regularly with fresh coats of paint, they are prone to rotting. Brickmold that isn't primed on both the front and back surfaces is particularly vulnerable to rot. If you are replacing your home's siding, have a close look at your current brickmold. Soft spots in the wood are telltale signs of rotting behind the paint. Rotting also occurs where the mitered molding meets in the corners. If you find rotted areas, replace the affected molding. You can remove and replace brickmold fairly easily and at any time, without removing siding.

Tools & Materials ▸

Pry bar	Caulk gun
Measuring tape	Brickmold
Pencil	Drip edge
Combination square	10d exterior
Miter saw	casing nails
Hammer and nail set	Caulk

How to Replace Damaged Brickmold

Remove old sections of brickmold with a pry bar. You may find it helpful to first insert a stiff-bladed paint scraper between the brickmold and underlying jamb to break the paint seal.

The best time to paint your new brickmold is before installing it. Prime all surfaces of the molding if it doesn't come preprimed, and paint the outer surfaces your trim color. Paint all your brickmold stock now in long strips.

Install drip edge. If no metal drip edge was in place above the old brickmold, cut a strip to length and slip it up into place behind the siding. Drip edge will extend the life of wood brickmold by keeping water from seeping behind it or soaking the ends.

4

Measure and cut strips of new brickmold to fit around the window or door. Miter-cut the top ends of the side pieces and both ends of the top piece at 45° using a miter saw. *Note: Some carpenters cut, fit, and nail one strip of brickmold at a time before miter-cutting the next piece. This way, you can adjust the miter angle slightly, if necessary, to improve the fit.*

5

Install the brickmold strips with 10d exterior casing nails driven every 12" into framing members. Use a nail set to drive the nail heads below the surface of the wood.

6

Seal the brickmold. Make sure the drip edge is tight against the top brickmold, then apply clear paintable silicone caulk along the top of the drip edge and along the outside edge of the side brickmold where it meets the siding. Fill the nail holes with caulk, and touch up these spots with paint.

Synthetic Brickmold ▸

These days, pine and fir aren't the only material options for brickmold and other exterior trim. You can also buy brickmold made of PVC or composites of resin, fiberglass, and wood pulp. Synthetic brickmold is about twice the price of wood brickmold, but it will last indefinitely, it is paintable, and it will not wick or hold water, which could rot surrounding framing. If you're willing to pay more for synthetics, the tradeoffs are worth the extra cost: you'll never have to maintain or replace your brickmold again.

Decorative Trim

If you are fortunate enough to live in a nineteenth-century Victorian home, you know how charming exterior trim can be. Whether theirs was a Stick, Queen Anne, Gothic, or Romanesque, our forebears measured their status, in part, by adorning their homes with all sorts of finery: fancy gable ends, brackets and corbels, fretwork, keystoned door and window surrounds, cornices, sunbursts, and miles of running molding.

Most of these trim details were made of wood, which means eventually you'll need to repair or replace them. Fortunately, there are numerous preservation sources for historic trimwork, and some millwork companies still specialize in manufacturing these architectural elements new. You can buy them made of wood or PVC plastic in a wide variety of styles and shapes.

You don't necessarily need to live in a Painted Lady in order to add a few of those decorative trim accents to your home. Consider installing fancy gable decorations and maybe some corbels under the soffits. Inject some life into a drab porch railing with turned balusters. Who knows? A splash of gingerbread trim could help your home become a more playful and eye-catching member of the block.

This Painted Lady's entryway is more than just a front door—it's a work of art, thanks to decorative trim details.

Trim Materials ▶

Gingerbread trim is manufactured in dozens of shapes and styles. The sampling shown here includes scrolled headers, a gable drop, niche surround, turned baluster, corbels, corner bracket, fretwork, gable decoration, and several samples of running molding.

One option for dressing up a gable is to make your own decorative headers. Draw your scrolled pattern onto a weather-resistant wood, such as cedar, redwood, or cypress. Cut out the header pieces with a jigsaw.

Screw your headers to flat strips of lumber for base pieces. Attach one header to each side of the gable with countersunk 3" deck screws. Leave room at the peak for inserting a gable drop with a turned finial on the tip.

You could also use a prefabricated gable decoration instead of scrolled headers and a drop. Gable decorations can be ordered to suit different roof pitches. Fasten them to the bottom edges of the fascia boards with countersunk 3" deck screws.

Custom Shutters

These customized shutters are designed to protect your windows from the high winds and flying debris of severe storms. Working exterior shutters are a permanent alternative to the frenzied rush of installing plywood over your windows in the hours before an approaching storm, only to have to remove it again once the danger has passed. For those of you far from the threat of coastal storms, working shutters provide a quick and easy way to protect the windows on summer cabins or cottages while you are away.

These easy-to-construct shutters are built from exterior-grade tongue and groove boards. Their simple, rustic design is offset with stylish beveled cleat-and-fan battens. A customized decorative trim, visible when open, can turn these utilitarian shutters into a fashionable complement to your home's exterior.

These customized shutters are designed to protect a window from the high winds and flying debris of a severe storm.

Tip ▸

"H" style lift-off hinge

"L" hinge and pintle

Lull and Porter mortise hinge

Strap hinge and pintle

Before you begin building your shutters, it is important to locate the proper hinges. Shutter hardware may not be readily available in all regions of the country and may have to be ordered from shutter manufacturers. Shutter hinges are available in a wide range of styles, and installation will vary depending upon the hinge and your window design. Always consult with the manufacturer to determine the hardware that will work best for your needs.

Tools & Materials ▸

Tape measure
Pipe clamps
Straightedge
Circular saw
Router with chamfer bit
Paintbrush
Drill
Wood glue
1 × 8 tongue and groove lumber
1 × 4 dimensional lumber
Galvanized deck screws (1¼", 3")
Paint
Shutter hardware

How to Build Custom Storm Shutters

To determine dimensions for your shutters, first measure the height of the window opening. Because windows may not be square, it's best to take both a right- and left-side measurement. Subtract ½" from the actual height to allow for clearance. To find the width of each shutter, measure the width between the inside edges of the window jamb, divide by two, and subtract ⅜" to allow for hinge clearance.

Assemble two to four tongue and groove 1 × 8s so that each shutter is slightly larger than its determined width. Hold the 1 × 8s together with pipe clamps, then use a straightedge to mark the dimensions on the face of each shutter. Cut the shutters to length using a circular saw.

Remove the clamps. Use a circular saw to rip the shutters to width, removing the grooved edge from one side of each shutter and the tongue edge from the other. Reattach the clamps.

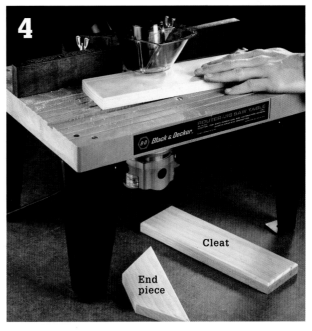

Cut four cleats 3" shorter than the shutter width from 1 × 4 exterior-grade lumber. Also cut four end pieces, mitering the ends at 45°. Bevel all edges that will not butt another piece using a router and chamfer bit.

(continued)

Attach the cleats and end pieces using waterproof wood glue and countersunk 1¼" galvanized screws. Allow glue to fully dry before installing the shutters.

Variation: To spruce up the simple design and construction of these shutters, consider a customized decorative trim design for the side that is visible when open. Ideas for trim include a sawtooth design or a traditional barn door Z- or X-style. Each design can be cut from 1 × 4 material and attached with wood glue and screws.

Paint or stain the shutters as desired and allow to dry. Drill pilot holes and attach the shutter hinges to the cleats with included fasteners or 1¼" galvanized screws.

Measure from the top of the shutter to the lower edge of the upper hinge and add ¼". Measure down this distance from the edge of the top jamb and make a mark. Align the bottom of the pintle's pin with the mark. Attach the pintle to the window molding using 3" galvanized screws.

8

9

Set the top hinge on the pintle. Support the shutter until both hinges are attached. Align the lower pintle with the lower hinge, and attach it with 3" galvanized screws. Repeat steps 7 and 8 for the other shutter. *Note: Hinge installation may vary due to hinge style and window design. Always follow manufacturer's directions.*

Install decorative holdbacks (also called shutter dogs) to hold the shutters in the open position. A slide latch can be installed inside or outside the shutters. An inexpensive alternative to latches is to install a pair of bar holders on the outside of the shutters and secure them with a 2 × 4 during a storm (inset).

Variation: Manufactured Storm Shutters

Manufactured storm shutters are available in many traditional styles, including louvered, raised panel, and board and batten.

Rolling shutters adjust to any position to provide storm protection or light control. They can be controlled manually or automatically.

Bahama-style shutters function as sun awnings when open and provide wind and impact protection when closed.

Painting & Staining Siding

Exterior painting and staining projects are inescapable for do-it-yourselfers. If you've just completed a wood siding project or added some wood trim details, the job isn't finished until you seal the wood with a protective top coat of stain or paint. Painting and staining seem like simple projects, but unless you prepare the surfaces properly by scraping, cleaning, and priming, you'll compromise the final top coat and shorten the life of your paint or stain—in some cases, dramatically.

Maybe you're simply intending to repaint or add a fresh coat of stain, but the current finish shows signs of problems. What do you do to correct the situation? This chapter will help you identify paint and stain problems, prepare surfaces properly for that first or next coat, and give you application options to make the job easier and faster. Painting and staining are relatively inexpensive ways to keep your home's exterior looking its best. These activities may not top your list of favorite projects, but when they're done correctly the results will last longer than you may think.

In this chapter:

- Tools & Materials
- Identifying Exterior Paint Problems
- Preparing to Paint
- Applying Primer & Paint
- Using Paint-Spraying Equipment
- Staining Siding

Tools & Materials

High-quality painting tools, primers, and paints usually produce better results with less work than less-expensive products. The return on an investment in quality products is a project that goes smoothly and results in an attractive, durable paint job.

Plan to prime all unpainted surfaces and any surfaces or patches that have been stripped or worn down to bare wood. For bare wood, the best approach is to apply one primer coat followed by two top coats.

But if the surface was previously painted and the old paint is still good, one coat of new paint is enough.

Although removing layers of old paint can be quite a chore, the proper materials can make the task go faster. If you don't own all of the specialty tools you need, such as a siding sander and heat gun, you can rent them at some home improvement stores and most rental centers. As you plan your painting project, make a list of the tools and materials you'll need.

Buy or rent a pressure washer and attachments to clean siding thoroughly and remove loose, flaky paint. Make sure to get the right unit. One with less than 1,200 psi won't do a good job, and one with more than 2,500 psi could damage your siding.

Tools for applying paint include roller and sleeve with ⅜" nap (A), corner roller (B), roller with ⅝" nap (C), 4" paintbrush (D), 3" paintbrush (E), 2" sash brush (F), 3"-wide roller (G). *Note: All brushes shown have synthetic bristles for use with latex-based paint.*

Materials for painting include painter's caulk (A), masonry, stucco, and brick paint (B), primer (C), house paint (D), drop cloth (E), plastic sheeting (F), epoxy wood filler (G), metal primer (H), masking tape (I), and 80-, 120-, and 150-grit sandpaper (J).

Products for surface preparation and maintenance include (from left) stripper for removing varnish, epoxy, and synthetic finishes; paint stripper for removing thick layers of paint; detergent; chlorine bleach for cleaning surfaces; muriatic acid for cleaning rust from metal; and trisodium phosphate (TSP).

Estimating Paint ▸

To estimate the amount of paint you need for one coat:

- Calculate the square footage of the walls (length × height), the square footage of the soffit panels and trim that will be painted, and add 15% waste allowance.
- Subtract from this figure the square footage of doors and windows.
- Check the paint coverage rate listed on the label (350 sq. ft. per gallon is average).
- Divide the total square footage by the paint coverage rate to determine the number of gallons you need.

Tools for paint removal include ⅓ sheet finish sander (A), drill with wire-wheel attachments (B), ¼ sheet palm sander (C), heat gun (D), caulk gun (E), steel wool (F), wire brushes (G), stiff-bristle brush (H), sanding blocks (I), paint scraper (J), paint zipper (K), painter's 5-in-1 tool (L), detail scraper (M), and putty knife (N).

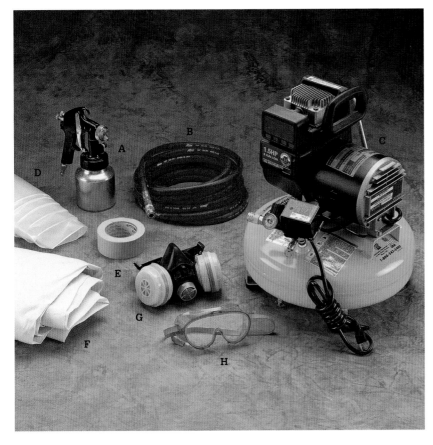

Paint-spraying equipment includes spray gun (A), hose (B), and compressor (C). Proper preparation requires plastic sheeting (D), masking tape (E), and drop cloths (F). Always use the necessary protective devices, including dual-cartridge respirator (G), and safety goggles (H).

Identifying Exterior Paint Problems

Two enemies work against painted surfaces—moisture and age. A simple leak or a failed vapor barrier inside the house can ruin even the finest paint job. If you notice signs of paint failure, such as blistering or peeling, take action to correct the problem right away. If the surface damage is discovered in time, you may be able to correct it with just a little bit of touch-up painting.

Evaluating the painted surfaces of your house can help you identify problems with siding, trim, roofs, and moisture barriers. The pictures on these two pages show the most common forms of paint failure and how to fix them. Be sure to fix any moisture problems before repainting.

Evaluate exterior painted surfaces every year, starting with areas sheltered from the sun. Paint failure will appear first in areas that receive little or no direct sunlight and is a warning sign that similar problems are developing in neighboring areas.

Common Forms of Paint Failure

Blistering appears as a bubbled surface. It results from poor preparation or hurried application of primer or paint. The blisters indicate trapped moisture is trying to force its way through the surface. To fix isolated spots, scrape and touch up. For widespread damage, remove paint down to bare wood, then apply primer and paint.

Peeling occurs when paint falls away in large flakes. It's a sign of persistent moisture problems, generally from a leak or a failed vapor barrier. If the peeling is localized, scrape and sand the damaged areas, then touch up with primer and paint. If it's widespread, remove the old paint down to bare wood, then apply primer and paint.

Alligatoring is widespread flaking and cracking, typically seen on surfaces that have many built-up paint layers. It can also be caused by inadequate surface preparation or by allowing too little drying time between coats of primer and paint. Remove the old paint, then prime and repaint.

Localized blistering and peeling indicates that moisture, usually from a leaky roof, gutter system, or interior pipe, is trapped under the paint. Find and eliminate the leak, then scrape, prime, and repaint the area.

Clearly defined blistering and peeling occurs when a humid room has an insufficient vapor barrier. If there's a clear line where an interior wall ends, remove the siding and replace the vapor barrier.

Mildew forms in cracks and in humid areas that receive little direct sunlight. Wash mildewed areas with a 1:1 solution of household chlorine bleach and water or with trisodium phosphate (TSP).

Rust occurs when moisture penetrates paint on iron or steel. Remove the rust and loose paint with a drill and wire brush attachment, then prime and repaint.

Bleeding spots occur when nails in siding begin to rust. Remove the nails, sand out the rust, then drive in galvanized ring-shank nails. Apply metal primer, then paint to blend in with the siding.

Efflorescence occurs in masonry when minerals leech through the surface, forming a crystalline or powdery layer. Use a scrub brush and a muriatic acid solution to remove efflorescence before priming and painting.

Preparing to Paint

The key to an even paint job is to work on a smooth, clean, dry surface—so preparing the surface is essential. Generally, the more preparation work you do, the smoother the final finish will be and the longer it will last.

For the smoothest finish, sand all the way down to the bare wood with a power sander. For a less time-consuming (but rougher) finish, scrape off any loose paint, then spot-sand rough areas. You can use pressure washing to remove some of the flaking paint, but by itself, pressure washing won't create a smooth surface for painting.

Tools & Materials ▸

Pressure washer
Scraper
Sander
Sanding block
Putty knife
Stiff-bristle brush
Wire brush
Steel wool
Coarse abrasive pad
Drill
Wire-wheel attachment

Caulk gun
Heat gun
Proper respiratory
   protection
Sandpaper (80-,
   120-, 150-grit)
Putty
Paintable
   siliconized caulk
Muriatic acid
Sealant

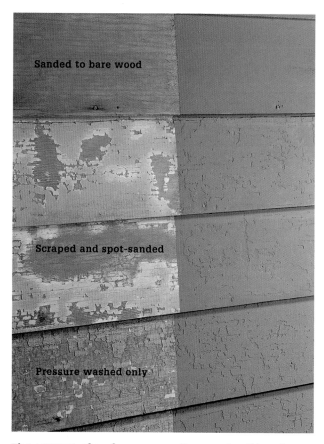

The amount of surface preparation you do will largely determine the final appearance of your paint job. Decide how much sanding and scraping you're willing to do to obtain a finish you'll be happy with.

How to Remove Paint

Use a heat gun to loosen thick layers of old paint. Aim the gun at the surface, warm the paint until it starts to bubble, then scrape the paint as soon as it releases.

To remove large areas of paint on wood lap siding, use a siding sander with a disk that's as wide as the reveal on your siding.

How to Prepare Surfaces for Paint

Clean the surface and remove loose paint by pressure washing the house. As you work, direct the water stream downward, and don't get too close to the surface with the sprayer head. Allow all surfaces to dry thoroughly before continuing.

Scrape off loose paint using a paint scraper. Be careful not to damage the surface by scraping too hard.

Smooth out rough paint with a finishing sander and 80-grit sandpaper. Use sanding blocks and 80- to 120-grit sandpaper to sand hard-to-reach areas of trim. *Tip: You can make sanding blocks from dowels, wood scraps, or garden hoses.*

Use detail scrapers to remove loose paint in hard-to-reach areas. Some of these scrapers have interchangeable heads that match common trim profiles.

Inspect all surfaces for cracks, rot, and other damage. Mark affected areas with colored pushpins or tape. Fill the holes and cracks with epoxy wood filler.

Use a finishing sander with 120-grit sandpaper to sand down repaired areas, ridges, and hard edges left from the scraping process, creating a smooth surface.

How to Prepare Window & Door Trim for Paint

Scuff-sand glossy surfaces on doors, window casings, and all surfaces painted with enamel paint. Use a coarse abrasive pad or 150-grit sandpaper.

Fill cracks in siding and gaps around window and door trim with paintable siliconized acrylic caulk.

How to Remove Clear Finishes

Pressure wash stained or unpainted surfaces that have been treated with a wood preservative or protectant before recoating them with fresh sealant.

Use a stiff-bristle brush to dislodge any flakes of loosened surface coating that weren't removed by pressure washing. Don't use a wire brush on wood surfaces.

How to Prepare Metal & Masonry for Paint

Remove rust and loose paint from metal hardware, such as railings and ornate trim, using a wire brush. Cover the surface with metal primer immediately after brushing to prevent the formation of new rust.

Scuff-sand metal siding and trim with medium-coarse steel wool or a coarse abrasive pad. Wash the surface and let dry before priming and painting.

Remove loose mortar, mineral deposits, or paint from mortar lines in masonry surfaces with a drill and wire-wheel attachment. Clean broad, flat masonry surfaces with a wire brush. Correct any minor damage before repainting.

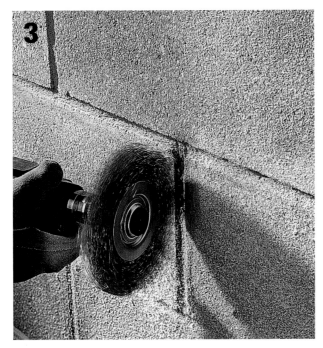

Dissolve rust on metal hardware with diluted muriatic acid solution. When working with muriatic acid, it's important to wear safety equipment, work in a well-ventilated area, and follow all manufacturer's directions and precautions.

Applying Paint & Primer

Schedule priming and painting tasks so that you can paint within two weeks of priming surfaces. If more than two weeks pass, wash the surface with soap and water before applying the next coat.

Check the weather forecast and keep an eye on the sky while you work. Damp weather or rain within two hours of application will ruin a paint job. Don't paint when the temperature is below 50° or above 90°F. Avoid painting on windy days—it's dangerous to be on a ladder in high winds, and wind blows dirt onto the fresh paint.

Plan each day's work so you can follow the shade. Prepare, prime, and paint one face of the house at a time, and follow a logical painting order. Work from the top of the house down to the foundation, covering an entire section before you move the ladder or scaffolding.

Tools & Materials ▸

Paintbrush (4", 2½", 3")	Primer
	House paint
Sash brush	Trim paint
Scaffolding	Cleanup materials
Ladders	

Paint in a logical order, starting from the top and working your way down. Cover as much surface as you can reach comfortably without moving your ladder or scaffolding. After the paint or primer dries, touch up any unpainted areas that were covered by the ladder or ladder stabilizer.

Tips for Applying Primer & Paint

Use the right primer and paint for each job. Always read the manufacturer's recommendations.

Plan your painting sequence so you paint the walls, doors, and trim before painting stairs and porch floors. This prevents the need to touch up spills.

Apply primer and paint in the shade or indirect sunlight. Direct sun can dry primers and paints too quickly and trap moisture below the surface, which leads to blistering and peeling.

Tips for Selecting Brushes & Rollers

Wall brushes, which are thick, square brushes 3 to 5" wide, are designed to carry a lot of paint and distribute it widely. *Tip: It's good to keep a variety of clean brushes on hand, including 2½", 3", and 4" flat brushes, 2" and 3" trim brushes, and tapered sash brushes.*

Trim and tapered sash brushes, which are 2 to 3" wide, are good for painting doors and trim, and for cutting in small areas.

Paint rollers work best for quickly painting smooth surfaces. Use an 8 or 9" roller sleeve for broad surfaces.

Use a 3" roller to paint flat-surfaced trim, such as end caps and corner trim.

Tips for Loading & Distributing Paint

Load your brush with the right amount of paint for the area you're covering. Use a full load of paint for broad areas, a moderate load for smaller areas and feathering strokes, and a light load when painting or working around trim.

Hold the brush at a 45° angle and apply just enough downward pressure to flex the bristles and squeeze the paint from the brush.

How to Use a Paintbrush

Load the brush with a full load of paint. Starting at one end of the surface, make a long, smooth stroke until the paint begins to feather out. *Tip: Paint color can vary from one can to the next. To avoid problems, pour all of your paint into one large container and mix it thoroughly. Pour the mixed paint back into the individual cans and seal them carefully. Stir each can before use.*

At the end of the stroke, lift the brush without leaving a definite ending point. If the paint appears uneven or contains heavy brush marks, smooth it out without overbrushing.

Reload the brush and make a stroke from the opposite direction, painting over the feathered end of the first stroke to create a smooth, even surface. If the junction of the two strokes is visible, rebrush with a light coat of paint. Feather out the starting point of the second stroke.

Tips for Using Paint Rollers

Wet the roller nap, then squeeze out the excess water. Position a roller screen inside a 5-gal. bucket. Dip the roller into the paint, then roll it back and forth across the roller screen. The roller sleeve should be full but not dripping when lifted from the bucket.

Cone-shaped rollers work well for painting the joints between intersecting surfaces.

Doughnut-shaped rollers work well for painting the edges of lap siding and moldings.

How to Paint Fascia, Soffits & Trim

Prime all surfaces to be painted, and allow ample drying time. Paint the face of the fascia first, then cut in paint at the bottom edges of the soffit panels. *Tip: Fascia and soffits are usually painted the same color as the trim.*

Paint the soffit panels and trim with a 4" brush. Start by cutting in around the edges of the panels using the narrow edge of the brush, then feather in the broad surfaces of the soffit panels with full loads of paint. Be sure to get good coverage in the grooves.

Paint any decorative trim near the top of the house at the same time you paint the soffits and fascia. Use a 2½" or 3" paintbrush for broader surfaces, and a sash brush for more intricate trim areas.

How to Paint Siding

Paint the bottom edges of lap siding by holding the paintbrush flat against the wall. Paint the bottom edges of several siding pieces before returning to paint the faces of the same boards.

Paint the broad faces of the siding boards with a 4" brush using the painting technique shown on page 222. Working down from the top of the house, paint as much surface as you can reach without leaning beyond the sides of the ladder.

Paint the siding all the way down to the foundation, working from top to bottom. Shift the ladder or scaffolding, then paint the next section. *Tip: Paint up to the edges of end caps and window or door trim that will be painted later.*

On board and batten or vertical panel siding, paint the edges of the battens, or top boards, first. Paint the faces of the battens before the sides dry, then use a roller with a ⅝"-nap sleeve to paint the large, broad surfaces between the battens.

How to Paint Stucco Walls

Using a large paintbrush, paint the foundation with antichalking masonry primer and let it dry. Using concrete paint and a 4" brush, cut in the areas around basement windows and doors.

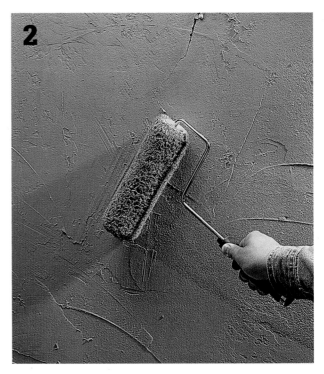

Apply concrete paint to board surfaces with a paint roller and a ⅝"-nap sleeve. Use a 3" trim roller or a 3" paintbrush for trim.

Tips for Cleaning Painting Tools

Scrape paint from roller covers with the curved side of a cleaner tool.

Use a spinner tool to remove paint and solvent from brushes and roller covers.

Comb brushes with the spiked side of a cleaner tool to properly align bristles for drying.

Cleaning Wood Siding ▸

Wood siding can provide a long and graceful service life, but it does require some routine maintenance to keep it looking its best. If your siding has a tinted stain finish, the effects of sunlight will slowly cause the color to fade. Eventually, the stain will lose its protective qualities, and the wood will turn silvery gray. Areas of your siding that do not receive direct sunlight are still prone to other problems. Shady areas can remain damp, which invites mold or algae growth and eventually rot.

The best way to combat fading and deterioration is to thoroughly clean your wood siding every couple of years and apply a fresh coat of stain. If your siding is faded but not discolored, you may be able to simply wash it down with soapy water to remove dirt and other debris, then stain it again. If the wood has turned gray but isn't deteriorated, use a commercial deck cleaner, followed by thorough washing to restore the original wood color. If there are signs of mold or algae growth, use a diluted mixture of trisodium phosphate or a biodegradable cleaning product applied with a pump sprayer to kill the growth. Scrub these areas thoroughly, then wash off the chemicals.

Before you begin, cover shrubbery, electrical outlets, and leaky doors or windows with plastic sheeting to protect them. Dampen plants under the sheeting to keep them from overheating in the sun. When using chemicals or pressure washing, be sure to wear safety glasses and protective clothing if required. Pressure wash judiciously using the proper wand tip. A pressure washer is an excellent cleaning tool, but it has the power to damage your siding if you're not careful.

Tools & Materials ▸

Garden hose and spray applicator or nozzle
Hand pump sprayer

Stiff-bristle push broom
Pressure washer (optional)

Plastic sheeting
Deck cleaner

Trisodium phosphate granules or biodegradable cleaner

Cleaning Tips

For routine cleaning: If your stain color has faded but the siding is in good condition, use a garden hose to wash off dirt or other debris. You can use a spray applicator and diluted mixture of mild detergent to clean off minor staining. Allow the siding to dry thoroughly for a day or two before restaining.

To revitalize weathered wood: You can usually restore the natural wood color of sun-faded cedar or redwood siding using a commercial deck cleaner formulated with a brightening agent. Apply it with a hand pump sprayer and let it soak in according to the manufacturer's instructions. You may need to follow the application by scrubbing the siding with a stiff-bristle push broom to work the chemicals into the wood.

Using Paint-Spraying Equipment

Spray equipment can make quick work of painting, but it still requires the same careful preparation work as traditional brush and roller methods. Part of that prep work involves using plastic to completely cover doors, windows, and other areas that you don't want painted, rather than just taping them off.

Spray equipment can be purchased or rented at hardware and home improvement stores. There are several types and sizes of spray equipment, including high-volume low-pressure (HVLP), airless, air-assisted airless, and electrostatic enhanced. They all work the same way—by atomizing paint and directing it to a worksurface in a spray or fan pattern. For our project, we used an HVLP sprayer, which we recommend because it produces less overspray and more efficient paint application than other sprayers.

Be sure to read and follow all safety precautions for the spray equipment. Since the paint is under a lot of pressure, it can not only tear the skin, but it can inject toxins into the bloodstream if used incorrectly. Wear the proper safety protection, such as safety glasses and a respirator, when spray painting the house.

As with other paint applications, pay close attention to the weather. Don't spray if rain is likely, and don't spray on windy days, since the wind can carry the paint particles away from the siding.

Tools & Materials ▸

Utility knife	Masking tape
Spray equipment	Plastic
Paint	Cardboard
Safety glasses	Cheesecloth
Respirator	5-gal. bucket

Paint sprayers allow you to cover large areas of siding and trim in a short amount of time. They also make it easier to paint areas that are hard to reach with a brush or roller.

How to Paint Using a Paint Sprayer

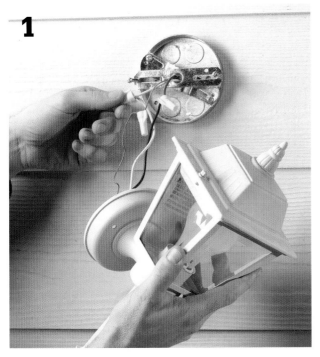

1

Remove outside light fixtures, window and door screens, and other detachable items that you don't want painted. Turn off power before disconnecting power to fixture.

2

Cover doors, windows, and any other areas you don't want painted using plastic and masking tape.

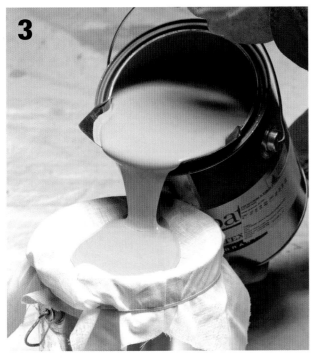

3

Strain the paint through cheesecloth to remove particles and debris. Mix the paint together in a 5-gal. bucket. Fill the sprayer container.

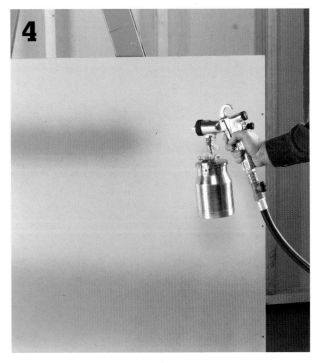

4

Spray a test pattern of paint on a scrap piece of cardboard. Adjust the pressure until you reach an even "fan" without any thick lines along the edge of the spray pattern.

(continued)

5

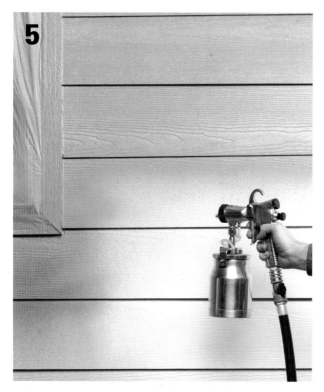

Cut in around doors and windows with the paint. Spray the paint along each side of the doors and windows, applying the paint evenly.

6

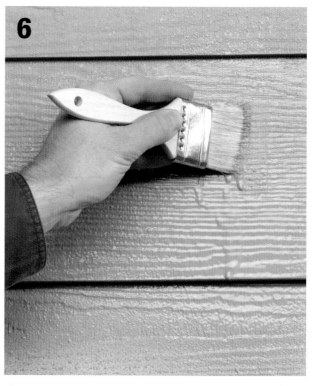

If you happen to spray an excessive amount of paint in an area and it starts to run, stop the sprayer. Use a paintbrush to spread out the paint and eliminate the runs.

7

Hold the spray gun perpendicular to the house, approximately 12" from the wall. Start painting near the top of the wall, close to a corner. Move your entire arm, rather than just the wrist, in a steady side-to-side motion. Do not wave your arm in an arc. Start your arm movement, then start the gun.

8

Spray the paint in an even motion, being careful not to tilt the gun. As you sweep your arm back and forth, overlap each coat of paint by 20 to 30 percent, working your way down the wall. When stopping, release the trigger before discontinuing your motion.

How to Paint Doors Using a Paint Sprayer

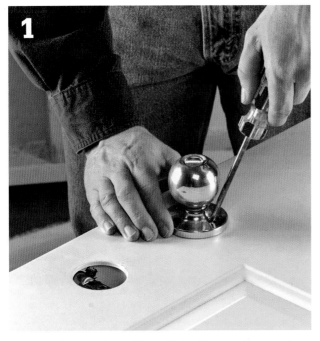

1

Remove the door by taking off the hinges. Remove all hardware from the door, such as handles and locks. If the door contains glass, you can either tape it off, or allow paint to get on the glass and then scrape it off with a razor after it's dry.

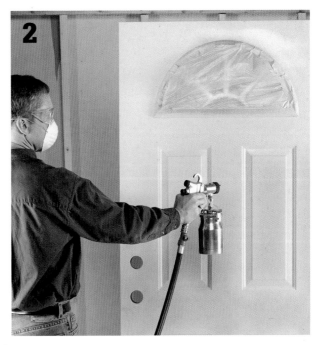

2

Prop up the door so it stands vertically. Starting at the top of the door, spray on the paint. As you make passes across the door, slightly go past the edges before sweeping back in the opposite direction. Wait until the paint is completely dry, then turn the door around and paint the other side.

Staining Siding

Stain lends color to wood siding, but because it is partially transparent, it also allows the natural beauty of the wood grain to show through. Water-based stains are applied with an acrylic or synthetic brush. Oil-based stains are usually applied with a natural-bristle brush.

Work in small sections at a time. Complete an entire length of board without stopping in the middle. Unlike paint, stain can darken or leave streaks if you go back over an area after it dries. Save the trim until the end, then stain it separately to get an even coverage.

Staining requires the same careful preparation work as painting. The surface must be clean and dry. Avoid working in direct sunlight so the stain doesn't dry too quickly. Check manufacturer's recommendations before staining. Some stains cannot be applied in temperatures below 50°F.

Tools & Materials ▸

Paintbrush
 or foam brush

Cloths
Stain

Exterior wood stain enhances color and protects wood. It requires renewing every 2 to 4 years.

| Solid-color stain | Semi-transparent stain | Transparent wood finish |

Exterior wood stain for siding or decks is sold in three primary formulations: solid, semi-transparent, and transparent.

Use an HVLP sprayer to apply stain to wood siding. Thin the stain if directed by the sprayer manufacturer.

Use a paint roller sleeve to apply stain to rough-textured surfaces, such as T1-11 siding. A long extension pole will let you reach well up the wall. Use a thick-nap sleeve (⅝" is shown here).

Roofing & Siding Repairs

Mother Nature can be cruel to your home's roofing and siding. Sunlight curls and cracks shingles and heavy winds come along and blow a few off. Moisture causes roof leaks in summer and adds thousands of pounds of ice and snow in the winter. Then, there are those unexpected catastrophes that occasionally happen: a storm drops a tree limb on the gutters, your little Major Leaguer hits a fly ball that dents the siding, or a persistent woodpecker decides to take up residence in your wood fascia. One way or the other, roof and siding repairs will eventually end up on your project list.

Take heart: this chapter will show you how to evaluate and then carry out a wide variety of roofing and siding repairs. Most of these projects can be completed in a day's time or less, so you can move on to more enjoyable pursuits. Even if you're not facing a repair situation right now, have a close look at these projects so you're ready when the time comes.

In this chapter:

- Inspecting & Repairing a Roof
- Cleaning Roofs
- Evaluating Siding & Trim
- Repairing Siding
- Repairing Masonry Walls
- Repairing Stucco Walls
- Repairing Wood Fascia & Soffits
- Repairing Gutters
- Repairing Trim

Inspecting & Repairing a Roof

A roof system is composed of several elements that work together to provide three basic, essential functions for your home: shelter, drainage, and ventilation. The roof covering and flashing are designed to shed water, directing it to gutters and downspouts. Air intake and outtake vents keep fresh air circulating below the roof sheathing, preventing moisture and heat buildup.

When your roof system develops problems that compromise its ability to protect your home—cracked shingles, incomplete ventilation, or damaged flashing—the damage quickly spreads to other parts of your house. Routine inspections are the best way to make sure the roof continues to do its job effectively.

Tips for Identifying Roofing Problems

Ice dams occur when melting snow refreezes near the eaves, causing ice to back up under the shingles, where it melts onto the sheathing and seeps into the house.

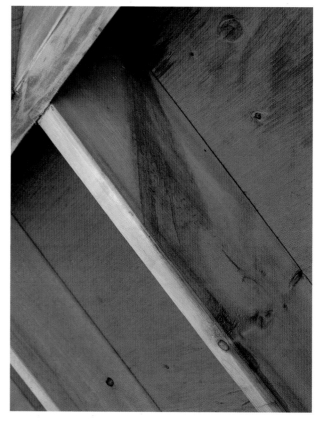

Inspect both the interior and the exterior of the roof to spot problems. From inside the attic, check the rafters and sheathing for signs of water damage. Symptoms will appear in the form of streaking or discoloration. A moist or wet area also signals water damage.

Common Roofing Problems

Wind, weather, and flying debris can damage shingles. The areas along valleys and ridges tend to take the most weather-related abuse. Torn, loose, or cracked shingles are common in these areas.

Buckled and cupped shingles are usually caused by moisture beneath the shingles. Loosened areas create an entry point for moisture and leave shingles vulnerable to wind damage.

A sagging ridge might be caused by the weight of too many roofing layers. It might also be the result of a more significant problem, such as a rotting ridge board or insufficient support for the ridge board.

Dirt and debris attract moisture and decay, which shorten a roof's life. To protect shingles, carefully wash the roof once a year using a pressure washer. Pay particular attention to areas where moss and mildew may accumulate.

In damp climates, it's a good idea to nail a zinc strip along the center ridge of a roof, under the ridge caps. Minute quantities of zinc wash down the roof each time it rains, killing moss and mildew.

Overhanging tree limbs drop debris and provide shade that encourages moss and mildew. To reduce chances of decay, trim any limbs that overhang the roof.

How to Locate & Evaluate Leaks

If you have an unfinished attic, examine the underside of your roof with a flashlight on a rainy day. If you find wetness, discoloration, or other signs of moisture, trace the trail up to where the water is making its entrance.

Water that flows toward a wall can be temporarily diverted to minimize damage. Nail a small block of wood in the path of the water, and place a bucket underneath to catch the drip. On a dry day, drive a nail through the underside of the roof decking to mark the hole.

If the leak is finding its way to a finished ceiling, take steps to minimize damage until the leak can be repaired. As soon as possible, reduce the accumulation of water behind a ceiling by poking a small hole in the wallboard or plaster and draining the water.

Once you mark the source of a leak from inside, measure from that spot to a point that will be visible and identifiable from outside the house, such as a chimney, vent pipe, or the peak of the roof. Get up on the roof and use that measurement to locate the leak.

How to Make Emergency Repairs

If your roof is severely damaged, the primary goal is to prevent additional damage until permanent repairs are made. Nail a sheet of plywood to the roof to serve as emergency cover to keep out the wind and water. *Tip: For temporary repairs, use double-headed nails, which can be easily removed. Fill nail holes with roofing cement when the repair is complete.*

Cover the damaged area by nailing strips of lath around the edges of a plastic sheet or tarp.

How to Make Spot Repairs with Roofing Cement

To reattach a loose shingle, wipe down the felt paper and the underside of the shingle. Let each dry, then apply a liberal coat of roofing cement. Press the shingle down to seat it in the bed of cement. *Tip: Heat softens the roof's surface, and cold makes it brittle. If needed, warm shingles slightly with a hair dryer to make them easier to work with and less likely to crack.*

Tack down buckled shingles by cleaning below the buckled area, filling the area with roofing cement, then pressing the shingle into the cement. Patch cracks and splits in shingles with roofing cement.

Check the joints around flashing, which are common places for roof leaks to occur. Seal any gaps by cleaning out and replacing any failed roofing cement.

How to Replace Asphalt Shingles

Pull out damaged shingles, starting with the uppermost shingle in the damaged area. Be careful not to damage surrounding shingles that are still in good condition.

Remove old nails in and above the repair area using a flat pry bar. Patch damaged felt paper with roofing cement.

Install the replacement shingles, beginning with the lowest shingle in the repair area. Nail above the tab slots using $7/8$ or 1" roofing nails.

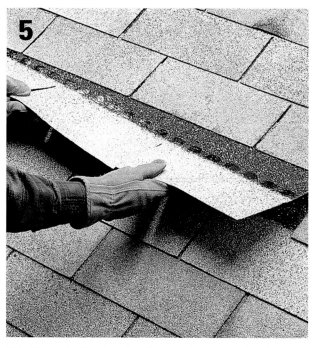

Install all but the top shingle with nails, then apply roofing cement to the underside of the top shingle, above the seal line.

Slip the last shingle into place, under the overlapping shingle. Lift the shingles immediately above the repair area, and nail the top replacement shingle.

How to Replace Wood Shakes & Shingles

Split the damaged wood shingles or shakes with a wood chisel and mallet so they can be removed.

Remove the pieces. Slide a hacksaw blade under the overlapping shingles and cut the nail heads. Pry out the remaining pieces of the shakes or shingles.

Gently pry up, but don't remove, the shakes or shingles above the repair area. Cut new pieces for the lowest course, leaving a ⅜" gap between pieces. Nail replacements in place with ring-shank siding nails. Fill in all but the top course in the repair area.

Cut the shakes or shingles for the top course. Because the top course can't be nailed, use roofing cement to fasten the pieces in place. Apply a coat of roofing cement where the shakes or shingles will sit, then slip them beneath the overlapping pieces. Press down to seat them in the roofing cement.

How to Replace Valley Flashing

Asphalt roofing is most prone to leaking where two roof planes meet—in the valleys. Sometimes the metal valley flashing is corroded or poorly nailed, producing a leak; or if your shingles are woven over one another in a valley, there may not be any underlying metal flashing at all. As soon as the shingles start to deteriorate, a leak is bound to happen. It could also be that your current metal flashing's design is redirecting water back under the shingles during heavy rains and creating leaks. Whatever the case may be, you may need to replace the flashing or improve how it's installed. If the current shingles are in good condition, you can do this project without replacing your entire roof.

The process for replacing valley flashing involves four main stages. First, you'll carefully remove the shingles in the valley area so they can be reinstalled over the new flashing later. Second, self-adhesive underlayment membrane is rolled onto the roof deck to provide a barrier beneath the metal flashing. This step ensures that roofing felt isn't your roof's only line of defense if the metal leaks in the future. Third, you'll install new W-style aluminum valley flashing, which will never corrode. Finally, the original shingles are laced back into place over the flashing and cut back to leave the flashing area partially exposed.

Tools & Materials ▸

Pry bar
Push broom
Hook-bladed
    utility knife
Measuring tape
Straightedge
Hammer
Aviation snips

Metal seamer
Chalk line
Self-adhesive
    underlayment
    membrane
Aluminum W-style
    valley flashing
Roofing nails

Before

After

Damaged valley flashing can be patched for temporary leak stoppage, but you should replace it completely as soon as you can.

How to Replace Damaged Valley Flashing

Carefully lift shingles in the valley area with a prybar to break their self-seal strip, and pry the nails free. Shingles are generally held in place with eight nails—four from the shingle above and four above the tabs. Slide the shingles out and stack them in order so they'll be easier to replace later. Remove enough shingles to completely expose the valley flashing.

Pry off the old flashing and remove all nails. Sweep the valley area thoroughly, clearing off all of the debris on the roof deck. Inspect the roofing felt and decking surfaces. If the felt is torn or the decking is deteriorated from moisture, replace it now. (For more on replacing sheathing, see pages 68 to 69.)

Roll out the self-adhesive underlayment membrane from the ridge to the eave with the paper backing facing down. You can use granulated or bare membrane for this application. Cut the membrane off the roll so it overlaps the eave and ridge.

Starting at the ridge, peel off the backing paper to expose the adhesive and stick the membrane down on the roofing felt. You may find it helpful to tack the membrane at the ridge to anchor it. Slip the membrane under any overhanging shingles as you proceed, and keep the membrane as flat and smooth as possible. It must make full contact with the deck and not be gapped at the base of the valley, or it could tear and breach the seal.

(continued)

5

Set the first piece of valley flashing in place so it overlaps the eave. Use a straightedge to mark cutting lines on the flashing that match the angles of the roof decks. The goal here is to cut the flashing about 1" longer than the end of the roof so you can lap the flashing over the drip edge. It will prevent ice dams from forming here in the winter.

6

Use a metal seamer to bend the flashing overlaps down over the drip edge. Cut tabs in the notched area of the flashing and fold them over the raised ridge to close this gap.

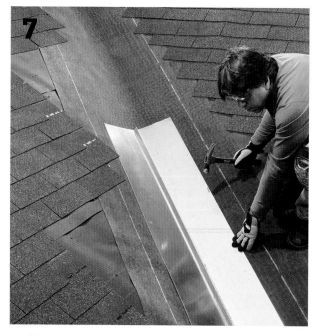

7

Position the eave flashing carefully, and nail it in place with ⅞" roofing nails spaced every 12" up the flashing. Drive the nails within 1" of the edge of the flashing only.

8

When the first strip of flashing is completely nailed, set the second strip in place on the roof deck so it overlaps the first by 1 ft. With assistance, stretch a chalk line from the eave to the ridge to make sure both flashings form a straight line along the center ridge. Make any adjustments to the fit, and proceed to nail the second strip to the deck. Continue to install flashing up to the ridge, and cut off the overhang with aviation snips.

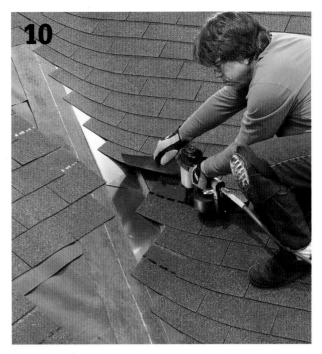

Slip the shingles back into position along one edge of the flashing from eave to ridge. Renail the shingles to the roof deck using the same nailing pattern as you would when installing them new.

Carefully lift the overlapping shingle edges, and nail the shingles to the valley flashing within 1" of its edge.

With an assistant's help, snap a chalk line from the ridge to the eave to mark a trim line on the overlapping shingles. Position this line so about 3" of the flashing next to the flashing ridge will be exposed at the roof ridge and about 6" will be exposed at the eave. The wider exposure of flashing at the bottom will help handle the greater volume of water here without overflowing the flashing.

Trim off the overhanging portion of each shingle along the chalk line to complete the first side of the flashing detail. Then repeat the process of refitting, nailing, marking, and trimming shingles on the other side of the flashing to finish the valley. Slip a scrap of wood behind the shingles to protect the flashing when trimming the shingles.

How to Replace Step Flashing

Carefully bend up the counter flashing or the siding covering the damaged flashing. Cut any roofing cement seals, and pull back the shingles. Use a flat pry bar to remove the damaged flashing. *Tip: When replacing flashing around masonry, such as a chimney, use copper or galvanized steel. Lime from mortar can corrode aluminum.*

Cut the new flashing to fit, and apply roofing cement to all unexposed edges. Slip the flashing in place, making sure it's overlapped by the flashing above and overlaps the flashing and shingle below.

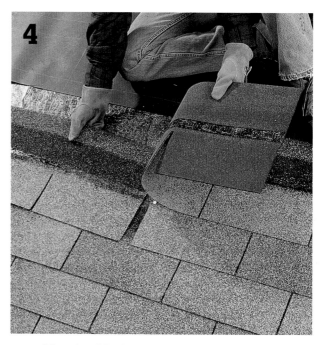

Drive one roofing nail through the flashing, at the bottom corner, and into the roof deck. Do not fasten the flashing to the vertical roof element, such as a chimney.

Reposition the shingles and counter flashing, and seal all joints with roofing cement.

Cleaning Roofs

If you live in a coastal region or on heavily wooded property, your asphalt roof may have discolored staining from mildew and algae growth. Provided these are just stains and not fungi or mold growth (signs of more serious moisture problems), you can remove the stains easily and have your roof looking new again. The process involves spraying the shingles with a solution of pool chlorine and liquid detergent, then rinsing it off with a garden hose. Chlorine will begin to kill the algae immediately and brighten the shingle color, but it will also continue to work for days after treating. Spray water onto shrubbery and the surrounding yard first, especially in downspout areas, to help dilute the chemical runoff.

Use extreme caution when walking on a wet roof. Wear soft-soled rubber sneakers for optimal traction, and protect yourself from the chlorine by wearing a rain suit and safety glasses. Choose a calm, overcast day for the job.

If your roof has a steep pitch, do not attempt this project; hire a professional roof-cleaning service to do the work instead.

Tools & Materials ▸

Ladder
Pump sprayer
Garden hose and
  spray nozzle

1 gal. of liquid
  pool chlorine
Liquid
  dish detergent

How to Clean an Asphalt Roof

Make the cleaner. Combine 1 gal. of swimming pool chlorine and 1 oz. of liquid dish detergent in a pump-style garden sprayer. Wear chemical gloves and safety glasses to protect yourself. *Tip: Spray your shrubs and yard with water to dilute any chemical overspray.*

Apply the cleaner. Working from the ridge to the eaves, apply the bleach solution with a garden sprayer in 6- to 10-ft. sections. Work quickly so the entire section can be rinsed clean while the treatment is still wet. Wear protective clothing, rubber-soled shoes, and safety glasses when working with the chemical spray.

Spray off the chemicals with a garden hose and clean water. Do not use a pressure washer for this step—it will blast granules off the shingles and shorten their life. Watch your step when working near the eaves. Follow up the first chemical spray and wash with a second application of a 50/50 mixture of chlorine and water. Rinse off the second treatment thoroughly with more fresh water before the chlorine dries.

Evaluating Siding & Trim

The first step in inspecting and evaluating siding and trim is to identify the type of material used on the house. Once you determine the material, take a close look at the problem area and determine the best method to fix it. If your siding is still under warranty, read through the warranty document before starting any repairs. Making repairs yourself could invalidate the product warranty. If the siding was professionally installed, you may want to talk to your contractor about the repairs.

In addition to looking unsightly, small siding problems can escalate into larger and more costly problems. As soon as you spot any siding damage, take steps to fix it immediately, especially if there's a possibility of water infiltration.

Check window and door trim for rot, especially on horizontal surfaces and at joints. Try to make repairs without removing the trim.

Tips for Inspecting Trim

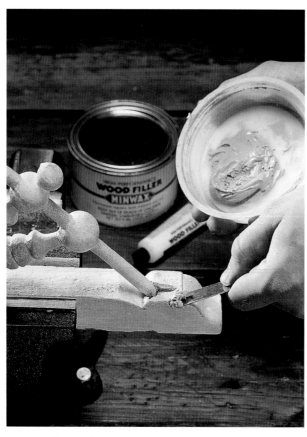

Inspect decorative trim, like the gingerbread trim shown here. If you suspect damage, remove the trim and make repairs in a workshop.

Evaluate broad trim pieces, such as the end cap trim shown above, and make repairs using the same techniques as for siding.

Common Siding Problems

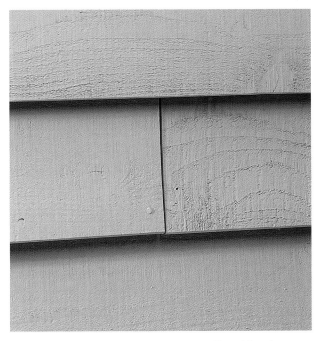

Separated joints can occur in any type of lap siding, but they're most common in wood lap. Gaps between ⅛ and ¼" thick can be filled with caulk. Gaps ⅜" or wider could mean that your house has a serious moisture or shifting problem. Consult a building inspector.

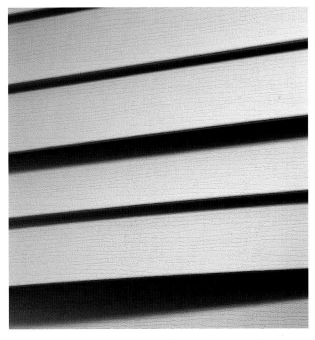

Buckling occurs most frequently in manufactured siding when expansion gaps are too small at the points where the siding fits into trim and channels. If possible, move the channels slightly to give the siding more room. If not, remove the siding, trim the length slightly, then reinstall.

Minor surface damage to metal siding is best left alone in most cases—unless the damage has penetrated the surface. With metal products, cosmetic surface repairs often look worse than the damage.

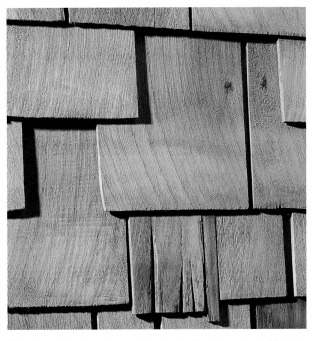

Missing siding, such as cedar shakes that have been blown away from the wall, should be replaced immediately. Check the surrounding siding to make sure it's secure.

Repairing Siding

Damage to siding is fairly common, but fortunately, it's also easy to fix. Small to medium holes, cracks, and rotted areas can be repaired with filler or by replacing the damaged sections with matching siding.

If you cannot find matching siding for repairs at building centers, check with salvage yards or siding contractors. When repairing aluminum or vinyl siding, contact the manufacturer or the contractor who installed the siding to help you locate matching materials and parts. If you're unable to find an exact match, remove a section of original siding from a less visible area of the house, such as the back of the garage, and use it for the patch. Cover the gap in the less visible area with a close matching siding, where the mismatch will be less noticeable.

Tools & Materials ▸

Aviation snips	Paintbrush
Caulk gun	Epoxy wood filler
Drill	Epoxy glue
Flat pry bar	Galvanized ring-
Hammer	shank siding nails
Straightedge	Siliconized
Tape measure	acrylic caulk
Utility knife	Roofing cement
Zip-lock tool	30# felt paper
Chisel	Sheathing
Trowel	Trim
Screwdrivers	Replacement siding
Hacksaw	End caps
Circular saw	Wood preservative
Jigsaw	Primer
Key hole saw	Paint or stain
Nail set	Metal sandpaper
Stud finder	

Nailing strip

J-channel

Shown cutaway for clarity

Vinyl and metal siding panels have a locking J-channel that fits over the bottom of the nailing strip on the underlying piece. Use a zip-lock tool (inset) to separate panels. Insert the tool at the seam nearest the repair area. Slide it over the J-channel, pulling outward slightly, to unlock the joint from the siding below.

How to Patch Vinyl Siding

Starting at the seam nearest the damaged area, unlock interlocking joints using a zip-lock tool. Insert spacers between the panels, then remove the fasteners in the damaged siding using a flat pry bar. Cut out the damaged area using aviation snips. Cut a replacement piece 4" longer than the open area, and trim 2" off the nailing strip from each end. Slide the piece into position.

Insert siding nails in the nailing strip, then position the end of a flat pry bar over each nail head. Drive the nails by tapping on the neck of the pry bar with a hammer. Place a scrap piece of wood between the pry bar and siding to avoid damaging the siding. Slip the locking channel on the overlapping piece over the nailing strip of the replacement piece. *Tip: If the damaged panel is near a corner, door, or window, replace the entire panel. This eliminates an extra seam.*

How to Patch Aluminum Siding

Cut out the damaged area using aviation snips. Leave an exposed area on top of the uppermost piece to act as a bonding surface. Cut a patch 4" larger than the repair area. Remove the nailing strip. Smooth the edges with metal sandpaper.

Nail the lower patch in place by driving siding nails through the nailing flange. Apply roofing cement to the back of the top piece, then press it into place, slipping the locking channel over the nailing strip of the underlying piece. Caulk the seams.

How to Replace Aluminum End Caps

Remove the damaged end cap. If necessary, pry the bottom loose, then cut along the top with a hacksaw blade. Starting at the bottom, attach the replacement end caps by driving siding nails through the nailing tabs and into the framing members.

Trim the nailing tabs off the top replacement cap. Apply roofing cement to its back. Slide the cap over the locking channels of the siding panels. Press the top cap securely in place.

How to Replace Board & Batten Siding

Remove the battens over the damaged boards. Pry out the damaged boards in their entirety. Inspect the underlying housewrap, and patch if necessary.

Cut replacement boards from the same type of lumber, allowing a ⅛" gap at the side seams. Prime or seal the edges and the back side of the replacement boards. Let them dry.

Nail the new boards in place using ring-shank siding nails. Replace the battens and any other trim. Prime and paint or stain the new boards to blend with the surrounding siding.

How to Replace Wood Shakes & Shingles

Split damaged shakes or shingles with a hammer and chisel, and remove them. Insert wood spacers under the shakes or shingles above the repair area, then slip a hacksaw blade under the top board to cut off any remaining nail heads.

Cut replacement shakes or shingles to fit, leaving a ⅛- to ¼"-wide gap at each side. Coat all sides and edges with wood preservative. Slip the patch pieces under the siding above the repair area. Drive siding nails near the top of the exposed area on the patches. Cover nail heads with caulk. Remove the spacers.

How to Replace Lap Siding

1 If the damage is caused by water, locate and repair the leak or other source of the water damage.

2 Mark the area of siding that needs to be replaced. Make the cutout lines over the center of the framing members on each side of the repair area, staggering the cuts to offset the joints. *Tip: Use an electronic stud finder to locate framing members, or look for the nail heads.*

3 Insert spacers beneath the board above the repair area. Make entry cuts at the top of the cutting lines with a key hole saw, then saw through the boards and remove them. Pry out any nails or cut off the nail heads using a hacksaw blade. Patch or replace the sheathing and building paper, if necessary.

4 Measure and cut replacement boards to fit, leaving an expansion gap of ⅛" at each end. Use the old boards as templates to trace cutouts for fixtures and openings. Use a jigsaw to make the cutouts. Apply wood sealer or primer to the ends and backs of the boards. Let them dry.

5 Nail the new boards in place with siding nails, starting with the lowest board in the repair area. At each framing member, drive nails through the bottom of the new board and the top of the board below. *Tip: If you removed the bottom row of siding, nail a 1 × 2 starter strip along the bottom of the patch area.*

6 Fill expansion joints with caulk (use paintable caulk for painted wood or tinted caulk for stained wood). Prime and paint or stain the replacement boards to match the surrounding siding.

Repairing Masonry Walls

Masonry repairs are doomed to fail if the underlying causes of the problems aren't addressed. For example, masonry bricks can separate if the structure is still being subjected to the stress that caused the original damage.

Pinpoint the nature and cause of the problems before you start repairs. Look for obvious clues, such as overgrown tree roots or damaged gutters that let water drain onto masonry surfaces. Also check the slope of the surrounding landscape to see if it needs to be regraded to direct water away from the foundation. After you're sure you've eliminated the problem, you're ready to repair the damage.

For walls with internal damaged areas, remove only the damaged section, keeping the upper layers intact if they are in good condition. Do not remove more than four adjacent bricks in one area—if the damaged area is larger, it will require temporary support, which is a job for a professional mason.

Tools & Materials ▸

Drill with a masonry-cutting disc
Mason's chisel
Hammer
Wire brush
Pointing trowel
Masonry trowel
Jointing tool
Mortar mix
Concrete fortifier
Mortar pigment

Types of Brick Problems

Deteriorating mortar joints are common and usually more widespread than surface deterioration of bricks. If you find damaged mortar, probe surrounding joints with a screwdriver to determine if they're sound. Tuck point deteriorating joints by removing cracked, damaged mortar, then filling the joints with fresh mortar.

Spalling occurs when trapped moisture is exposed to repeated freeze and thaw cycles, exerting enough directional pressure to fracture bricks. If the damage is contained to a fairly small area, you can replace only the affected bricks (opposite page). If the problem is more widespread, the structure may have to be replaced.

How to Replace Damaged Brick

Use an angle grinder with a masonry-cutting disc to score lines on the damaged brick and in the surrounding mortar joints.

Break the brick apart along the scored lines using a masonry chisel and hammer. If removing several bricks, work from the top down, one row at a time. Be careful not to damage surrounding bricks.

Chisel out any mortar remaining in the cavity, then brush away dirt and debris using a wire brush. Rinse the area with water. *Tip: Save fragments from broken bricks to use as color references when shopping for replacement bricks.*

Mix the mortar, adding concrete fortifier and, if necessary, pigment to match the old mortar. Use a pointing trowel to apply a 1"-thick layer of mortar to the bottom and sides of the cavity.

Dampen the replacement brick slightly, then apply mortar to the ends and top. Fit the brick into the cavity and tap it with the handle of the trowel until the face is flush with the surrounding bricks. If needed, press more mortar into the joints using a pointed trowel.

Scrape away excess mortar with a masonry trowel. Smooth the joints using a jointing tool that matches the profile of the surrounding joints. Let the mortar set until crumbly, then brush away any excess.

Repairing Stucco Walls

Although stucco siding is very durable, it can be damaged, and over time it can crumble or crack. The directions given below work well for patching small areas less than two sq. ft. For more extensive damage, the repair is done in layers, as shown on the opposite page.

Tools & Materials ▸

Caulk gun	Metal primer
Disposable	Stucco patching
paintbrush	compound
Putty knife	Bonding adhesive
Mason's trowel	Denatured alcohol
Square-end trowel	Metal primer
Hammer	Stucco mix
Whisk broom	Masonry paint
Wire brush	1½" roofing nails
Masonry chisel	15# building paper
Aviation snips	Self-furring metal lath
Pry bar	Masonry caulk
Drill with masonry bit	Tint
Scratching tool	Metal stop bead

Fill thin cracks in stucco walls with masonry caulk. Overfill the crack with caulk and feather until it's flush with the stucco. Allow the caulk to set, then paint it to match the stucco. Masonry caulk stays semiflexible, preventing further cracking.

How to Patch Small Areas

Remove loose material from the repair area using a wire brush. Use the brush to clean away rust from any exposed metal lath, then apply a coat of metal primer to the lath.

Apply premixed stucco repair compound to the repair area, slightly overfilling the hole using a putty knife or trowel. Read manufacturer's directions, as drying times vary.

Smooth the repair with a putty knife or trowel, feathering the edges to blend into the surrounding surface. Use a whisk broom or trowel to duplicate the original texture. Let the patch dry for several days, then touch it up with masonry paint.

How to Repair Large Areas

Make a starter hole with a drill and masonry bit, then use a masonry chisel and hammer to chip away stucco in the repair area. *Note: Wear safety glasses and a particle mask or respirator when cutting stucco. Cut self-furring metal lath to size and attach it to the sheathing using roofing nails. Overlap pieces by 2". If the patch extends to the base of the wall, attach a metal stop bead at the bottom.*

To mix your own stucco, combine three parts sand, two parts Portland cement, and one part masonry cement. Add just enough water so the mixture holds its shape when squeezed (inset). Mix only as much as you can use in 1 hour. *Tip: Premixed stucco works well for small jobs, but for large ones, it's more economical to mix your own.*

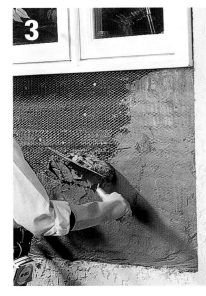

Apply a ⅜"-thick layer of stucco directly to the metal lath. Push the stucco into the mesh until it fills the gap between the mesh and the sheathing. Score horizontal grooves into the wet surface using a scratching tool. Let the stucco dry for two days, misting it with water every 2 to 4 hours.

Apply a second, smooth layer of stucco. Build up the stucco to within ¼" of the original surface. Let the patch dry for two days, misting every 2 to 4 hours.

Combine finish coat stucco mix with just enough water for the mixture to hold its shape. Dampen the patch area, then apply the finish coat to match the original surface. Dampen the patch periodically for a week. Let it dry for several more days before painting.

Repairing Wood Fascia & Soffits

Fascia and soffits add a finished look to your roof and promote a healthy roof system. A well-ventilated soffit system prevents moisture from building up under the roof and in the attic.

Most fascia and soffit problems can be corrected by cutting out sections of damaged material and replacing them. Joints between fascia boards are lock nailed at rafter locations, so you should remove whole sections of fascia to make accurate bevel cuts for patches. Soffits can often be left in place for repairs.

Fascia and soffits close off the eaves area beneath the roof overhang. The fascia covers the ends of rafters and rafter lookouts, and provides a surface for attaching gutters. Soffits are protective panels that span the area between the fascia and the side of the house.

Tools & Materials ▸

Circular saw
Jigsaw
Drill
Putty knife
Hammer
Flat pry bar
Nail set
Chisel
Caulk gun
Paintbrush

Replacement
    materials
Nailing strips
Galvanized deck
    screws (2", 2½")
4d galvanized
    casing nails
Acrylic caulk
Primer
Paint

How to Repair Wood Fascia

Remove gutters, shingle moldings, and any other items mounted on the fascia. Carefully pry off the damaged fascia board using a pry bar. Remove the entire board and all old nails.

Set your circular saw for a 45° bevel, and cut off the damaged portion of the fascia board. Reattach the undamaged original fascia to the rafters or rafter lookouts using 2" deck screws. Bevel-cut a patch board to replace the damaged section.

Set the patch board in place. Drill pilot holes through both fascia boards into the rafter. Drive nails in the holes to create a locknail joint (inset). Replace shingle moldings and trim pieces using 4d casing nails. Set the nail heads. Prime and paint the new board.

How to Repair Wood Panel Soffits

In the area where soffits are damaged, remove the support moldings that hold the soffits in place along the fascia and exterior wall. Drill entry holes, then use a jigsaw to cut out the damaged soffit area. *Tip: Cut soffits as close as possible to the rafters or rafter lookouts. Finish cuts with a chisel, if necessary.*

Remove the damaged soffit section using a pry bar. Cut nailing strips the same length as the exposed area of the rafters, and fasten them to the rafters or rafter lookouts at the edges of the openings using 2½" deck screws.

Using soffit material similar to the original panel, cut a replacement piece ⅛" smaller than the opening. If the new panel will be vented, cut the vent openings.

Attach the replacement panel to the nailing strips using 2" deck screws. If you are not going to paint the entire soffit after the repair, prime and paint the replacement piece before installing it.

Reattach the soffit molding using 4d casing nails. Set the nail heads.

Using siliconized acrylic caulk, fill all nail holes, screw holes, and gaps. Smooth out the caulk with a putty knife until the caulk is even with the surface. Prime and paint the soffit panels.

Repairing Gutters

Gutters perform the important task of channeling water away from your house. A good gutter system prevents damage to your siding, foundation, and landscaping, and it helps prevent water from leaking into your basement. When gutters fail, evaluate the type and extent of damage to select the best repair method. Clean your gutters and downspouts as often as necessary to keep the system working efficiently.

Tools & Materials ▶

Flat pry bar
2 hacksaw
Caulk gun
Pop rivet gun
Drill
Hammer
Stiff-bristle brush
Putty knife
Steel wool
Aviation snips
Level
Paintbrush
Trowel
Garden hose

Chalk line
Wood scraps
Replacement
   gutter materials
Siliconized
   acrylic caulk
Roofing cement
Metal flashing
Sheet-metal screws
   or pop rivets
Gutter hangers
Primer and paint
Gutter patching kit
Gutter guards

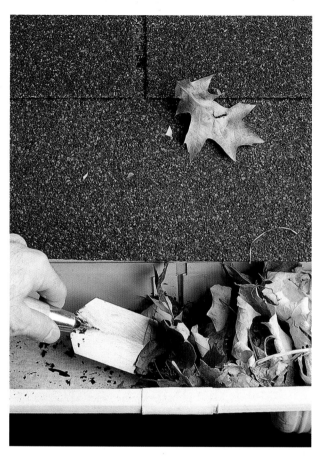

Use a trowel to clean leaves, twigs, and other debris out of the gutters before starting the repairs.

Keep gutters and downspouts clean so rain falling on the roof is directed well away from the foundation. Nearly all wet basement problems are caused by water collecting near the foundation, a situation that can frequently be traced to clogged and overflowing gutters and downspouts.

How to Unclog Gutters

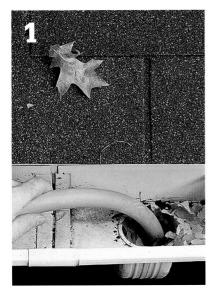

Flush clogged downspouts with water. Wrap a large rag around a garden hose and insert it in the downspout opening. Arrange the rag so it fills the opening, then turn on the water full force.

Check the slope of the gutters using a level. Gutters should slope slightly toward the downspouts. Adjust the hangers, if necessary.

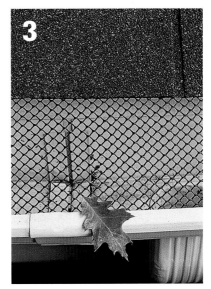

Place gutter guards over the gutters to prevent future clogs.

How to Rehang Sagging Gutters & Patch Leaks

For sagging gutters, snap a chalk line on the fascia that follows the correct slope. Remove hangers in and near the sag. Lift the gutter until it's flush with the chalk line. *Tip: A good slope for gutters is a ¼" drop every 10 ft. toward the downspouts.*

Reattach hangers every 24" and within 12" of seams. Use new hangers, if necessary. Avoid using the original nail holes. Fill small holes and seal minor leaks using gutter caulk.

Use a gutter patching kit to make temporary repairs to a gutter with minor damage. Follow manufacturer's directions. For permanent repairs, see pages 194 to 197.

How to Repair Leaky Joints

Drill out the rivets or unfasten the metal screws to disassemble the leaky joint. Scrub both parts of the joint with a stiff-bristle brush. Clean the damaged area with water, and allow to dry completely.

Apply caulk to the joining parts, then reassemble the joint. Secure the connection with pop rivets or sheet-metal screws.

How to Patch Metal Gutters

Clean the area around the damage with a stiff-bristle brush. Scrub it with steel wool or an abrasive pad to loosen residue, then rinse it with water.

Apply a ⅛"-thick layer of roofing cement evenly over the damage. Spread the roofing cement a few inches past the damaged area on all sides.

Cut and bend a piece of flashing to fit inside the gutter. Bed the patch in the roofing cement. Feather out the cement to reduce ridges so it won't cause significant damming. *Tip: To prevent corrosion, make sure the patch is the same type of metal as the gutter.*

How to Replace a Section of Metal Gutter

Remove gutter hangers in and near the damaged area. Insert wood spacers in the gutter near each hanger before prying. *Tip: If the damaged area is more than 2 ft. long, replace the entire section with new material.*

Slip spacers between the gutter and fascia near each end of the damaged area, so you won't damage the roof when cutting the gutter. Cut out the damaged section using a hacksaw.

Cut a new gutter section at least 4" longer than the damaged section.

Clean the cut ends of the old gutter using a wire brush. Caulk the ends, then center the gutter patch over the cutout area and press into the caulk.

Secure the gutter patch with pop rivets or sheet-metal screws. Use at least three fasteners at each joint. On the inside surfaces of the gutter, caulk over the heads of the fasteners.

Reinstall gutter hangers. If necessary, use new hangers but don't use old holes. Prime and paint the patch to match the existing gutter.

Repairing Trim

Some exterior trim serves as decoration, like gingerbread and ornate cornice moldings. Other trim, such as brickmold and end caps, works with siding to seal your house from the elements. Damaged brickmold and corner boards should be patched with stock material similar to the original.

If you cannot find matching replacement parts for decorative trim at home improvement stores, check salvage shops or contact a custom millworker.

Tools & Materials ▸

Hammer
Chisel
Circular saw
Nail set
Putty knife
Utility knife
Paintbrush
Flat pry bar
Caulk gun
Epoxy wood filler
Epoxy glue

Caulk
10d galvanized casing nails
Galvanized ring-shank siding nails
Sandpaper
Paint
Building paper
Drip edge
Replacement trim

Repair delicate or ornamental trim molding in your workshop whenever possible. You'll get better results than if you try repairing it while it's still attached.

Tips for Repairing & Replacing Trim

Reattach loose trim with new ring-shank siding nails driven near old nail locations. Fill old nail holes with paintable caulk, and touch up caulk and new nail heads with paint to match the surrounding surface.

Repair decorative trim molding with epoxy glue or wood filler. For major repairs, make your own replacement parts, or take the trim to a custom millwork shop.

How to Replace Brickmold

Pry off old brickmold around windows and doors using a flat pry bar. Remove any old drip edge. Inspect and repair the building paper.

Hold a replacement piece of brickmold, slightly longer than the original piece across the opening. Mark cutting lines to fit the opening. Cut the replacement molding at the marks, matching any miter cuts.

Cut a 3"-wide piece of flashing to fit between the jambs, then bend it in half lengthwise to form the new drip edge (preformed drip edge is also available). Slip it between the siding and building paper, above the door or window. Do not nail the drip edge in place.

Test-fit the replacement piece of brickmold, then apply exterior-grade panel adhesive to the back side. Follow the manufacturer's directions for allowing the adhesive to set.

Nail the brickmold to the door header using 10d galvanized casing nails. Locknail the miter joints and set all nail heads. Seal joints and cover nail holes with caulk. Prime and paint when the caulk dries.

Conversion Charts

Lumber Dimensions

Nominal - U.S.	Actual - U.S. (in inches)	Metric	Nominal - U.S.	Actual - U.S. (in inches)	Metric
1 × 2	¾ × 1½	19 × 38 mm	1½ × 4	1¼ × 3½	32 × 89 mm
1 × 3	¾ × 2½	19 × 64 mm	1½ × 6	1¼ × 5½	32 × 140 mm
1 × 4	¾ × 3½	19 × 89 mm	1½ × 8	1¼ × 7¼	32 × 184 mm
1 × 5	¾ × 4½	19 × 114 mm	1½ × 10	1¼ × 9¼	32 × 235 mm
1 × 6	¾ × 5½	19 × 140 mm	1½ × 12	1¼ × 11¼	32 × 286 mm
1 × 7	¾ × 6¼	19 × 159 mm	2 × 4	1½ × 3½	38 × 89 mm
1 × 8	¾ × 7¼	19 × 184 mm	2 × 6	1½ × 5½	38 × 140 mm
1 × 10	¾ × 9¼	19 × 235 mm	2 × 8	1½ × 7¼	38 × 184 mm
1 × 12	¾ × 11¼	19 × 286 mm	2 × 10	1½ × 9¼	38 × 235 mm
1¼ × 4	1 × 3½	25 × 89 mm	2 × 12	1½ × 11¼	38 × 286 mm
1¼ × 6	1 × 5½	25 × 140 mm	3 × 6	2½ × 5½	64 × 140 mm
1¼ × 8	1 × 7¼	25 × 184 mm	4 × 4	3½ × 3½	89 × 89 mm
1¼ × 10	1 × 9¼	25 × 235 mm	4 × 6	3½ × 5½	89 × 140 mm
1¼ × 12	1 × 11¼	25 × 286 mm			

Metric Conversions

To Convert:	To:	Multiply by:	To Convert:	To:	Multiply by:
Inches	Millimeters	25.4	Millimeters	Inches	0.039
Inches	Centimeters	2.54	Centimeters	Inches	0.394
Feet	Meters	0.305	Meters	Feet	3.28
Yards	Meters	0.914	Meters	Yards	1.09
Square inches	Square centimeters	6.45	Square centimeters	Square inches	0.155
Square feet	Square meters	0.093	Square meters	Square feet	10.8
Square yards	Square meters	0.836	Square meters	Square yards	1.2
Ounces	Milliliters	30.0	Milliliters	Ounces	.033
Pints (U.S.)	Liters	0.473 (Imp. 0.568)	Liters	Pints (U.S.)	2.114 (Imp. 1.76)
Quarts (U.S.)	Liters	0.946 (Imp. 1.136)	Liters	Quarts (U.S.)	1.057 (Imp. 0.88)
Gallons (U.S.)	Liters	3.785 (Imp. 4.546)	Liters	Gallons (U.S.)	0.264 (Imp. 0.22)
Ounces	Grams	28.4	Grams	Ounces	0.035
Pounds	Kilograms	0.454	Kilograms	Pounds	2.2

Counterbore, Shank & Pilot Hole Diameters

Screw Size	Counterbore Diameter for Screw Head (in inches)	Clearance Hole for Screw Shank (in inches)	Pilot Hole Diameter Hard Wood (in inches)	Pilot Hole Diameter Soft Wood (in inches)
#1	.146 (%4)	5/64	3/64	1/32
#2	¼	3/32	3/64	1/32
#3	¼	7/64	1/16	3/64
#4	¼	1/8	1/16	3/64
#5	¼	1/8	5/64	1/16
#6	5/16	9/64	3/32	5/64
#7	5/16	5/32	3/32	5/64
#8	3/8	11/64	1/8	3/32
#9	3/8	11/64	1/8	3/32
#10	3/8	3/16	1/8	7/64
#11	½	3/16	5/32	9/64
#12	½	7/32	9/64	1/8

Adhesives

Type	Characteristics	Uses
White glue	**Strength:** moderate; rigid bond **Drying time:** several hours **Resistance to heat:** poor **Resistance to moisture:** poor **Hazards:** none **Cleanup/solvent:** soap and water	**Porous surfaces:** Wood (indoors) Paper Cloth
Yellow glue (carpenter's glue)	**Strength:** moderate to good; rigid bond **Drying time:** several hours; faster than white glue **Resistance to heat:** moderate **Resistance to moisture:** moderate **Hazards:** none **Cleanup/solvent:** soap and water	**Porous surfaces:** Wood (indoors) Paper Cloth
Two-part epoxy	**Strength:** excellent; strongest of all adhesives **Drying time:** varies depending on manufacturer **Resistance to heat:** excellent **Resistance to moisture:** excellent **Hazards:** fumes are toxic and flammable **Cleanup/solvent:** acetone will dissolve some types	**Smooth & porous surfaces:** Wood (indoors & outdoors) Metal Masonry Glass Fiberglass
Hot glue	**Strength:** depends on type **Drying time:** less than 60 seconds **Resistance to heat:** fair **Resistance to moisture:** good **Hazards:** hot glue can cause burns **Cleanup/solvent:** heat will loosen bond	**Smooth & porous surfaces:** Glass Plastics Wood
Cyanoacrylate (instant glue)	**Strength:** excellent but with little flexibility **Drying time:** a few seconds **Resistance to heat:** excellent **Resistance to moisture:** excellent **Hazards:** can bond skin instantly; toxic, flammable **Cleanup/solvent:** acetone	**Smooth surfaces:** Glass Ceramics Plastics Metal
Construction adhesive	**Strength:** good to excellent; very durable **Drying time:** 24 hours **Resistance to heat:** good **Resistance to moisture:** excellent **Hazards:** may irritate skin and eyes **Cleanup/solvent:** soap and water (while still wet)	**Porous surfaces:** Framing lumber Plywood and paneling Wallboard Foam panels Masonry
Water-base contact cement	**Strength:** good **Drying time:** bonds instantly; dries fully in 30 minutes **Resistance to heat:** excellent **Resistance to moisture:** good **Hazards:** may irritate skin and eyes **Cleanup/solvent:** soap and water (while still wet)	**Porous surfaces:** Plastic laminates Plywood Flooring Cloth
Silicone sealant (caulk)	**Strength:** fair to good; very flexible bond **Drying time:** 24 hours **Resistance to heat:** good **Resistance to moisture:** excellent **Hazards:** may irritate skin and eyes **Cleanup/solvent:** acetone	**Smooth & porous surfaces:** Wood Ceramics Fiberglass Plastics Glass

Converting Temperatures

Convert degrees Fahrenheit (F) to degrees Celsius (C) by following this simple formula: Subtract 32 from the Fahrenheit temperature reading. Then, mulitply that number by $5/9$. For example, $77°F - 32 = 45$. $45 \times 5/9 = 25°C$.

To convert degrees Celsius to degrees Fahrenheit, multiply the Celsius temperature reading by $9/5$. Then, add 32. For example, $25°C \times 9/5 = 45$. $45 + 32 = 77°F$.

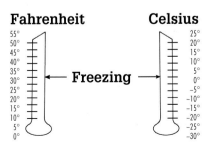

Resources

AGI Group, Inc.
800 823 6677
www.decorativeshutters.com

Alcoa Home Exteriors, Inc.
800 962 6973
www.alcoahomes.com

Alside
800 922 6009
www.alside.com

Alcoa
888 ALCOA 123
www.alcoa.com

The Brick Industry Association
703 620 0010
www.bia.org

CertainTeed Corporation
800 782 8777
www.certainteed.com

Clay Tile
MCA Superior Clay Roof Tile
800 736 6221
Www.mca-tile.com

Cultured Stone, Corp.
800 255 1727
www.culturedstone.com

DaVinci
800 328 4624
www.davinciroofscapes.com

Dupont
800 44-TYVEK
www.tyvek.com

Easy Heat, Inc.
800 537 4732
www.easyheat.com

GAF Materials Corporation
973 628 3000
www.gaf.com

James Hardie® Siding Products
866 4-Hardie
www.jameshardie.com

La Habra Stucco
877 547 8822
www.lahabrastucco.com

MCA Superior Clay Roof Tile
800 736 6221
www.mca-tile.com

Metal Roofing Alliance
360 275 6164
www.metalroofing.com

MetalWorks
800 320 0101
www.metalworksroof.com

Midwest Lumber
800 862 6003
www.midwestlumberinc.com

Monier Life Tile
800 571 8453
www.monierlifetile.com

National Roofing Contractors Association (NRCA)
847 299 9070
www.nrca.net

Novabrik
866 678 2745
www.novabrik.com

Owens Corning, Masonry Products, LLC
800 255 1727
www.culturedstone.com

ProtectoWrap
877 271 9661
www.protectowrap.com

Roof Depot, Inc.
800 458 8534
www.roofdepot.com

Roof Tile Institute
888 321 9236
www.rooftile.org

The Tapco Group
Mid-America Siding Components, The Foundry, Inspire Roofing Products, Atlantic Premium Shutters, Wellcraft, Builders Edge, Vantage, Stonecraft
800 771 4486
www.tapcoint.coms

Vande Hey Raleigh
920 766 0156
www.crmtile.com

Vinyl Siding Institute
888 367 8741
www.vinylsiding.org

Wellington Polymer Technology, Inc.
Enviroshake® composite engineered roofing (maintenance-free alternative to cedar) is 95% derived from recycled materials and carries a 50-year, non-prorated warranty.
866 423 3302
www.enviroshake.com

Western Red Cedar Lumber Association
604 684 0266
www.wrcla.org

Western Wood Products Association
503 224 3930
www.wwpa.org

Wheatbelt, Inc.
800 264 5171
www.rollupshutter.com

Photography Credits

AGI Group
p. 209 (lower left & lower right) photos courtesy of AGI Group

Alamy
p. 35 photo © David Hoffman Photo Library, Alamy / www. alamy.com; 42 (left) photo © Alamy / www.alamy.com

Alcoa Home Exteriors, Inc.
p. 11 (top left), 22–23 (all), 26, 38, 44 (top), 47, 118, 183 (lower left) photos courtesy of Alcoa

Alside
p. 12 (all), 13 (lower), 21 (top), 36, 72, 183 (middle right), 183 (middle right), 188 (lower left) photos courtesy of Alside

Andrea Rugg
p. 6 (lower), 32 (lower), 37 photos © Andrea Rugg

Beth Singer
p. 152 photo © Beth Singer

CertainTeed, Corp.
p. 16, 24, 46 (lower left), 74 photos courtesy of Certain Teed, Corp.

Clay Tile
p. 9 (lower), 30, 104 photos courtesy of Clay Tile

DaVinci
p. 10 (lower), 29 photos courtesy of DaVinci

FR Midwest
p. 9 (top right), 146 photos courtesy of FR Midwest

Gary Russ
p. 9 (top left) photo © Gary Russ

GAF Materials, Corp.
p. 27, 70, 86, 96 photos courtesy of GAF Materials, Corp.

Istock
p. 13 photo (top) © Jan Paul Schrage, Istock / www.istock. com; 14 photo © Istock / www.istock.com; 33 photo © Newton Page, Istock / www.istock.com; 41 photo © Greg Nicholas, Istock / www.istock.com; 180 photo © Istock / www.istock.com; 204 photo © Jyeshern Cheng, Istock / www.istock.com; 210 photo © / Frances Twitty, Istock / www.istock.com

James Hardie®
p. 140 photo courtesy of James Hardie® Siding Products

Jessie Walker
p. 7 (top), 90, 134 photos © Jessie Walker

Karen Melvin
p. 208 photo (top right) © Karen Melvin

La Habra Stucco
p. 6 (top), 172 photos courtesy of La Habra Stucco

Monier Life
p. 31, 34 (top) photos courtesy of Monier Life

Novabrik
p. 8 (top), 43 (lower), 166 photos courtesy of Novabrik

Owens Corning
p. 11 (top right & lower), 43 (top), 162 photos courtesy of Owens Corning

ProtectoWrap
p. 116 (top) photos courtesy of ProtectoWrap

Mark Samu
p. 60, 108 photos © Mark Samu

Scot Zimmerman
p. 4, 40 (left), 190 (left) photos © Scot Zimmerman

The Tapco Group
p. 3 Inspire Roofing Products, 7 (lower two) Mid-American Components, 8 (lower) StoneCraft, 21 The Foundary, 39 The Foundary, 42 (lower right)—all photos courtesy of The Tapco Group

Wellington Technology
p. 10 (top), 34 (lower) photos Wellington Technology

Wheatbelt, Inc.
p. 209 (lower middle) photo courtesy of Wheatbelt, Inc.

Index